The Dawn of
Professional
Golf

*To my father, who passed his
love of sports to me.*

The Dawn of *Professional Golf*

The Genesis of the European Tour
1894–1914

Peter N. Lewis

Hobbs & McEwan
New Ridley, Northumberland
&
Glengarden, Ballater

Oast Books
Tunbridge Wells

Copyright ©1995 Peter N. Lewis

First published in 1995
by Hobbs and McEwan,
New Ridley, Northumberland, and
Glengarden, Ballater, Aberdeenshire,
AB35 5UB
and by
Oast Books, 12 Dene Way, Speldhurst,
Tunbridge Wells, Kent TN3 0NX

All rights reserved. No part of this publication may be reproduced or transmitted in any form or by any means, electronic or mechanical, including photocopying, recording, or stored in any information storage or retrieval system, without either prior permission in writing from the publisher or a licence permitting restricted copying.

Edited by Michael Hobbs
Illustrations: Hobbs Golf Collection, British Golf Museum, and Sotheby's

Design: Rhod McEwan
Keyboarding: Margaret Hobbs

Created by
Three's Company,
12 Flitcroft Street,
London WC2H 8DJ

ISBN 1-898594-22-8

Printed in England by Martins the Printers, Berwick upon Tweed

Front endpaper: Tournament at Olton Park, 1910.

Back endpaper: The English team in 1903, including five Open champions.

Contents

Preface	*6*
Introduction: Setting the Scene	*7*
1. A New Ball and the Loss of Some Clubs	*17*
2. The Birth of the PGA	*31*
3. Exhibition Matches	*43*
4. High-stake Matches, 1894-1914	*57*
5. International Tours and Matches Abroad	*73*
6. Tournaments	*93*
7. The Open Championship	*103*
8. Major PGA Tournaments	*129*
9. European Opens	*149*
Epilogue	*155*
Appendices	
1. Exhibition Matches	*159*
2. Tournaments	*162*
3. Prize Money and Types of Matches	*166*
4. Growth of Golf Clubs	*168*
5. Results of Major Championships and Tournaments	*169*
Bibliography	*172*
Index	*173*

Preface

This book would not have been possible without the support of the Council of Management of the Royal & Ancient Golf Club of St Andrews Trust, who govern the British Golf Museum, and in particular the support of Ronnie Alexander and Tom Bisset. I would also like to thank my staff at the museum – Fiona Grieve, Katie Page, Hilary Webster and Grace Donald – for all their help. I am indebted to the Royal & Ancient Golf Club of St Andrews for allowing me access to their library. Preliminary studies that led to this full-scale work were published in *Golfiana*, and I would like to thank Bud Dufner, the editor, for his encouragement.

I would also like to thank David Anderson, Ian Morrison and my brother, Jim Lewis, for their help with computers, spread-sheets and databases, and Ted Toms and Graeme Dawson for their help with photographic material.

On a personal level, I must thank my wife, Liz, who did not complain too much about my spending virtually every Sunday at the office, researching and writing the book, and who gave me much support, encouragement and not too many household chores. At this point I had better mention my two children, Michael and Kathryn, who, now that they are old enough to read, will be very upset if they don't see their names in print.

Peter N. Lewis
British Golf Museum
St Andrews, 1995

Introduction

Setting the Scene

J.H. Taylor, 1894.

PROFESSIONAL GOLF HAS COME A VERY LONG WAY IN 100 YEARS. In 1994 there were 37 tournaments on the European PGA Volvo Tour, offering £19,186,155 in prize money, an average of £518,545 per tournament. This excludes the special events, such as the Alfred Dunhill Cup, the Toyota World Match Play Championship and the Johnnie Walker World Championship (£4,359,669 in prize money), the Challenge Tour (£1,767,111 in prize money) and the Seniors' Tour (£921,000 in prize money). The situation was very different in 1894, when there were 13 tournaments which offered a *total* purse of £469.50p, an average of £36.12p per tournament. Even allowing for inflation since 1894, that is a mighty great leap – from an average purse of £36.12p to £518,545! In 1894 only the Open Championship offered a purse of more than £50. With total prize money of £100, it was easily the most lucrative tournament of the year. Yet this sum, again even allowing for inflation, is a far cry from the £1,100,000 played for at Turnberry in 1994. Yet it all had to begin somewhere. Hidden somewhere in the mists of time is the origin of today's tour.

Some dates to remember

Historians, such as myself, tend to be very fond of dates. But dates can be very arbitrary. Why start looking at the development of professional golf in 1894? Why not 1860, when the first Open was played? Why not 1892, when the Open was first played over 72 holes? Why not 1901, when the PGA was founded? 1894 seemed to me to be as good a year as any. It was the year the Open was first played in England. It was the year an English professional first won the Open. These may appear strange reasons to come from somebody who lives in Scotland, even if I am an American. The significance of 1894 is that a gentleman named J.H. Taylor won the first of his five Open Championships. Taylor, along with Harry Vardon and James Braid, came to dominate and symbolise professional golf up until 1914. Their heyday coincides with an unprecedented growth of the game both in Britain and abroad, a growth which they helped to fuel.

It was in this 21-year period, 1894-1914, that the professional game was transformed from an annual series of random tournaments, of which the Open Championship was the only constant, to an almost regular tour,

Willie Auchterlonie, c. 1893.

dominated by PGA-run tournaments, but also including regular participation in tournaments in Europe and occasional forays to America. By understanding the change that the professional underwent between 1894 and 1914, one can begin to discern the genesis of the modern professional game. It still had to undergo much evolution after 1914, but the process had most definitely begun.

1914 is a date that many other historians are fond of using as a terminal date. It is used with considerably more justification than my rather arbitrary starting date. World War I began in August 1914. When that war ended in 1918, Europe was a very different place from what it had been.

At the start of 1894, golf in Britain was enjoying unprecedented growth. There were 716 clubs in existence in the four home countries of England, Scotland, Ireland and Wales plus the Isle of Man and the Channel Islands, of which 356 clubs were in England and 301 in Scotland. 529 of these clubs had courses attached to them. A decade earlier, in 1884, there had been a total of only 147 clubs in the entire United Kingdom.

There was as yet no single body responsible for the rules of the game; the R & A Rules of Golf Committee was not formed until 1897. There were no restrictions on the form and make of golf clubs – these would not come until 1909. The golf ball was equally unregulated, and there would be no rules governing its size and weight until 1920. A player could carry as many, or as few, clubs as he or she wished; there would be no rules about that until 1939.

The Open Championship, after the early years, was run under the auspices of a consortium of clubs, and had been played since 1860 while the Amateur Championship had been run since 1886. (It too was run by a consortium of clubs.) The R & A took over the running of these two championships in February 1920.

In 1894 the defending Open champion, Willie Auchterlonie, was 21 years old. Of the past champions who were professionals, Hugh Kirkaldy was still

From left to right: Hugh Kirkaldy, Willie Park junior and Willie Fernie (Open champion, 1883).

Hilton and Ball in the late 1890s.

only 25, Willie Park 29, David Brown 33, Jack Burns 34 and Willie Fernie 36. Three great professionals destined never to win the Open Championship, Ben Sayers, Andrew Kirkaldy and Douglas Rolland, who were 36, 33 and 33 respectively. Hugh Kirkaldy was to die young, while Willie Auchterlonie and Willie Park were to become increasingly preoccupied by their business interests. Alex (Sandy) Herd, who was already making a name for himself, was 25. On the horizon was the trio of players who were to dominate professional golf up to 1914 – J.H. Taylor, Harry Vardon and James Braid, who were 22, 23 and 23 years old respectively. Of the other golfers who were to feature prominently in the next two decades, Jack White was 20, while Arnaud Massy and Ted Ray were only 16, and George Duncan 10.

The only two Englishmen who had won the Open prior to 1894 were the great amateur players, John Ball and Harold Hilton. The Open had always been played in Scotland, but that was about to change with the 1894 championship being scheduled for Sandwich.

Although golfers could be well pleased with the rapid spread of their beloved game up to 1893, this was to turn out to be only the appetiser. By 1914, there were 2,844 clubs in the United Kingdom, and the number of clubs with courses had increased to 1,801. There were over 1,872 courses altogether, allowing for public courses and clubs with more than one course.

In 1890 there was no Professional Golfers' Association, and Horace Hutchinson wrote in the Badminton Library volume *Golf* that there were three ways that a man could "derive a precarious subsistence from the game of golf". These were as club-makers, "professional players who eked out existence by work in club-makers' shops" and "professional caddies who would be professional players if they played well enough".

Horace Hutchinson.

In 1894 there were 83 recorded professional matches and tournaments, and in 1913, the last full season before the war, there were 178. Until the formation of the PGA in 1901, there was no body to look after the interests of professionals, and tournaments, with the exception of the Open, were held on a random and haphazard basis. By 1914, the situation had changed considerably and the role of the professional at both club level and playing level had been greatly enhanced. At club level, the number of professional jobs had increased along with the number of clubs with courses, and thus about 1,200 new professional jobs were created, compared with the 500 jobs in existence at the beginning of 1894. Good performances in major tournaments gave professionals the exposure they needed either to be invited to play in exhibition matches, or move on to a bigger club. The leading professionals, in turn, now had the opportunity to play comparatively regularly in tournaments in Britain and Europe, and in the increasing number of exhibition matches.

The number of patents relating to golf equipment increased dramatically as man continued his search for the perfect club and the perfect ball that would make his shots fly far and straight and keep his putts on line and for hole. Some 97 patents had been registered at the Manchester Patent Library up till 1893. 711 patents were then registered between 1894 and 1914. Of these, 249 were for clubs, clubheads, shafts or grips, and 240 for balls or ball manufacture.

There were two major developments concerning golfing equipment between 1894 and 1914. These were the introduction of the rubber-cored ball, and the advent of rules concerning the form and make of golf clubs, which restricted some of the more creative clubs that had found their way on to the market.

The growth of sports

This dramatic increase in the popularity of all aspects of golf did not take place in isolation. It has often been written that the introduction of the gutta-percha ball in the 1850s was the reason that golf became popular. An early advocate of this idea was Horace Hutchinson, who wrote in 1897, that "with the introduction of the gutty ball, a comparatively durable article at a shilling [5p] or nine pence [37.5p], the game was at once brought within the means of many."[1] However, a look at the figures indicates that this is not the case. In 1851 there were about 24 clubs in the whole of Britain. This increased to 39 by 1860, 60 by 1870 and 98 by 1879. Dramatic increases began around 1887 and by 1889 there were 290 clubs. The gutta-percha ball was a tool that enabled the expansion to take place when other conditions were ripe – but it was not the cause.

The rising popularity of golf was part of a massive social change that took place in Britain in the second half of the nineteenth century. It was this social change, which in turn was fuelled by the advent of the railway and later other forms of transport, which was the catalyst for the increased popularity of golf.

The development of the railway system between 1830 and 1870 was staggering. In 1837 there were 1,500 miles of track in Britain, and this increased to 15,600 miles by 1870. With the basic railway system in place, it then spread to less-populated areas, with branch lines adding another 4,400 miles to the network by 1890. The railway broke down many social and physical barriers, as all classes of people were able to travel countrywide. Hutchinson, in his 1897 article, cited the railways as the chief agent in the change of national attitudes towards athletic pastimes.

In the 1880s, the safety bicycle had been introduced, providing a cheap form of transport for both men and women and, by the turn of the century, the motor car was beginning to become a factor in the growth of transport. In turn, roads and public transport systems developed in the major cities, especially in and around London.

Concurrent with these developments, the social impact of the industrial revolution had reached a peak by the 1870s. Many agricultural workers left the land and took up posts in business and commerce. As a result, cities throughout the country greatly expanded. Between 1871 and 1881 the population in towns and cities increased by 20%, as compared to 7% in the country. In 1877, agricultural prices began a collapse from which they would not recover in the period, giving further incentive to the growth of cities.

Out of this social change there emerged a vastly increased middle class of professional workers: doctors, lawyers, accountants, engineers, teachers, draughtsmen, book-keepers and clerks, who now led urban and suburban lives. The industrial working classes were also affected by changing lifestyles and even they had leisure time. Social legislation of the 1870s saw their work time reduced to 55 hours, allowing for a half-day off on Saturday afternoons and the introduction of four bank holidays in England.

This in turn led to a new attitude towards sports. There was a shift away from the traditional field sports, and organised games had become virtually compulsory in the rapidly growing number of public schools, where it was felt that sports were an important part of the moulding of a British gentleman.

Organised sports as we know them today emerged out of all this change. The Football Association was formed in 1863, and the Scottish Football Association was formed a decade later in 1873; the English Football League came into being in 1888, and the Scottish two years later in 1890. The Rugby Football Union was formed in 1871 and the Scottish in 1874. The Northern Rugby Football Union, later to be known as the Rugby League, broke away from the RFU in 1895.

In 1874, Major Wingfield patented a game called Sphairistike, which rapidly became known as lawn tennis. The game underwent major rules changes in 1877, and the first Wimbledon Championship was held that same year. 1877 also saw the first international cricket match between England and Australia. Cricket was seeing a transition from sporadic county matches and itinerant travelling teams to a county championship by the 1890s, with the MCC taking responsibility for overseeing the championship in 1895.

The paradox of the long history, but recent popularity, of golf is neatly summed up by C.G. Heathcote in the Badminton Library volume *Tennis, Lawn Tennis, Rackets, Fives* (1890): "Even golf, the newest madness of recent years, was chartered by royalty and practised by a little band of worshippers

Advertisement for a golfer's motor-cycle.

for two centuries and a half before, in these last days, it claimed a home on every common, forced a club into every hand, and deposited a ball in every bunker."

The spread of golf in Britain

All these social and economic factors combined to help fuel the great golf boom. There was a great interest in sports in general, and the improved transport made it easier and quicker to reach the countryside locations from the city.

Although the first patent for a lawn mower was taken out in October 1830, and the first licence for manufacture issued to J.R. & A. Ransome of Ipswich in 1832, mowers do not seem to have been used very much for either golf courses or cricket fields until 50 years later. But mowers were to prove vital to help maintain all the new courses being built.

One major factor that contributed to the growing popularity of the game was its enthusiastic endorsement by Arthur Balfour, a leading politician, and prime minister from 1902 to 1905. A report in 1898, which covered the opening of the Dorset Golf Club by Balfour, summed this up when it stated "It is to the devotion of Mr. Balfour and other distinguished and able men to the game that much of its ever increasing popularity is due." Balfour himself, in his speech at the club, said "More and more people are beginning to discover that there is no better way of spending a holiday, no more reasonable or

Arthur Balfour.

less elaborate method of enjoying a day's outing than playing good golf on good links." He went on to say that a drawback of the great popularity of the game was that in the summer courses were so crowded that a round of golf was often more conducive to the study of nature than the pursuit of golf, and that more courses were therefore needed.[2] And of course more were being built.

The great golf boom began to pick up momentum in the Jubilee Year of 1887 and continued right up to the outbreak of war in 1914. There has been much confusion in recent years over the number of golf clubs and societies in existence in the United Kingdom up to 1914. Most of this has been caused by a glaring error in Henderson's and Stirk's book, *Golf in the Making,* which gives a figure of 4,135 for the year 1910. This was taken from the editor's introduction of the 1909/10 volume of *Golfing Annual,* and is in fact the figure for all clubs, worldwide, listed in that volume. The true figure for 1910 should be about 729. There then comes the problems of how many courses went with these clubs and societies, and indeed how one defines a club as opposed to a society.

The problem of ownership of courses is almost impossible to resolve. I defined a club as having a course if *Golfing Annual* and *Nisbet's Golf Year* both list a club as having a course attached to it. I suggest three basic classes of clubs/societies: those which have courses attached to them; ladies' clubs, which are almost always a branch of a larger club; and city golfing societies, which would not have their own course. Courses in turn divide into three groups: those associated with a club, those which are clearly public courses (mainly in Scotland) and ladies' courses. There are undoubtedly overlaps between the first two groups, but these are not critical to the overall figures.

Thus in 1889 there was a total of 290 clubs, of which 206 are defined as having their own course, 33 were city golfing societies (CGS) and 22 ladies' clubs. The remaining clubs are those that did not have a course and were neither ladies' clubs nor CGS. In addition, there were over 16 public courses not included in the 'own club' classification, all in Scotland.

Of the 1914 total, 1,474 of the clubs were in England, 1,022 in Scotland, 125 in Wales, 206 in Ireland and 17 in the Channel Islands and the Isle of Man.

The same general pattern is followed for clubs with courses. At the end of 1889, there were 106 clubs with courses in England, 85 in Scotland, 2 in Wales and 9 in Ireland – a total of 206. By 1894 these totals had risen to 317, 157, 12, 37 respectively, plus 9 for the Channel Islands and Isle of Man, giving a total of 532. By 1914 the totals had reached 1,100 in England, 422 in Scotland, 104 in Wales, 163 in Ireland and 12 in the Channel Islands and Isle of Man.

In England, the geographic distribution of the 1,100 clubs with courses is not unexpected, 29% being in South East England and the Home Counties, 11% in Lancashire and 10% in Yorkshire. The rest were fairly evenly spread out. The growth of city golfing societies was largely a Scottish development between 1890 and 1914. Up to 1889 there were 33 in Scotland and none elsewhere. By 1914 there were 417 in Scotland, compared with 89 in

England, 9 in Ireland and one in Wales. 271 were in Edinburgh, compared with 70 in Glasgow and 53 in London.

In 1890 there were 30 clubs and 18 courses listed as specifically for ladies. These were almost all attached to men's clubs. By 1914 this had increased to ladies' 479 clubs and 51 had courses of their own.

Of the 1,872 courses identified up to 1914 and listed between 1909 and 1914, the number of holes is known for 1,859. 16 had fewer than 9 holes, 1,039 had 9 holes, 22 had between 10 and 17 holes and 782 had 18 holes. Thus in 1914, over half of the golf courses in the UK still had 9 holes rather than 18 holes.

Not every one was pleased with this rapid expansion of the number of golf courses. A Scottish golfer signing himself "Baffy" wrote to *Golf* in 1895: "Golf is attempted to be played in many places in England on ground about as fitted for the game as a summer fallow is for a game of cricket. We are all aware that one cannot make a silk purse out of a sow's ear or a proper golf links out of an old park, or fields of good inland pasture."[3]

This was apparently a widely held view, and in 1900 Horace Hutchinson argued against the notion that good golf could not be learned on inland courses. He pointed out that Taylor, Vardon, Braid and Herd were all based at, and practised at, inland courses. He also felt that "after coming from an inland green the golf on the seaside course appears relatively an easy game. The mashie slips under the ball so nicely, the ball lies up on the links turf so pleasantly."[4]

There simply was not enough available land by the seaside to cope with the demand for golf, nor were most golfers willing, or able, to travel to the coast for their game. In his book *Inland Golf*, published in 1915, Ted Ray estimated that 90% of all golf was played on inland courses.

Investing in golf

With this expansion in the sport, there was a massive amount of money being invested in golf. In 1899, Garden Smith estimated that £2,680,000 was being spent on golf per annum.[5] H. Ross Coubrough in 1904 estimated that 89,000 acres of land, with a rental value of £82,140, were being used for golf. He thought there were now about 168,725 golfers in Britain.[6] In 1905 Henry Leach wrote that £12,000 had been spent on the new public course in Bournemouth, £20,000 on the new course for Tooting Bec Golf Club and £6,000 for the new course at North Berwick.[7] *The Field* in June 1900 estimated that £10,000,000 had been invested in golf; but this figure was challenged by the editor of *Golf Illustrated* as perhaps too high.

Golf courses could have a very positive financial impact on the local community. In the financial year ending May 15th, 1900, the Corporation of Musselburgh collected £1,484.15p in green fees. The *Blackpool Herald* carried an article in May 1900 on the economic effect of golf in Blackpool and Lytham and St Anne's: "Golf has not only built hotels or enabled them to be built, but it has built boarding houses and club houses and made them into paying concerns. We have people taking furnished houses or buying or building houses that they may live near to good links. Golf has made St Annes; it is now making Fairhaven."

Membership of one of the major golf clubs was an expensive proposition. According to the 1893/94 *Golfing Annual,* the two most expensive clubs to join were Sandwich and Tooting Bec, at £15.75p each. The two highest annual subscriptions were at Neasden, at £6.30p, and Eltham, at £5.25p. By 1914 the highest was Royal Liverpool's entry fee, at £21, followed by the Royal & Ancient and Prestwick, at £20 each. Although Neasden had dropped its entry fee from £10.50 in 1894 to £5.25p, it had increased its annual subscription to £7.35p.

H.S.C. Everard, writing in 1897, estimated that it would cost a golfer £42.70p for a season of golf. This excluded club membership, subscriptions and green fees. After consulting with Willie Auchterlonie, he reckoned a set of three woods, three irons and a putter would come to £2. A bag would cost 20p; a dozen balls a week for 30 weeks £18, and 12.5p for a caddie per round for the same period £22.50.

Nine years later a discussion in an article in *Golf Illustrated* estimated that a day's golf cost 70p, on a pro rata basis for clubs, balls and fees. When travel and clothing were added, it took the average cost of a day's golfing to £1. The article concluded: "Yet if it must be admitted that golf costs money, there are few players who will deny that it is well worth it. We have never yet met a golfer who really grudged its expense." But it did admit that "golf as played today by the average club member is certainly not a poor man's game."[9]

Golf was widely perceived as an expensive game everywhere except in Scotland. Saxon Browne, writing in 1906, pointed out that "in no country as yet, except Scotland, have the lower classes shown any enthusiasm or aptitude for golf, the reason, of course, being that facilities for the game have not yet been afforded them, nor has the prevailing opinion that golf is an expensive game suitable only for the moneyed and leisured classes yet been exploded."[10] It was these moneyed and leisured classes that the professional golfer served at his club. In common with the other major sports, and cricket in particular, there was a great gap between gentlemen and players. Even the most successful professional golfers relied on the patronage of amateur players. The social barriers between the professionals and amateurs would only start to be breached in the inter-war period.

NOTES
1. *Golf,* August 6th, 1897
2. *Golf,* November 25th, 1898
3. *Golf,* July 29, 1895
4. *Golf Illustrated,* July 6th, 1900
5. *The Cost of Sport,* 1899.
6. *Golf Illustrated,* February 26th, 1904
7. *Golf Illustrated* December 29th, 1905
8. *Golf,* March 26th, 1897
9. *Golf Illustrated,* July 20th, 1906
10. *Golf Illustrated,* November 23rd, 1906

1. A New Ball and the Loss of Some Clubs

A new ball

ONE OF THE MAJOR DEVELOPMENTS to have a profound effect at all levels of the game was the change from the gutta-percha to the rubber-cored ball. This change was an important contributor to the continuing growth of golf up to 1914. The gutta-percha, or gutty, ball had been in use since the 1850s, when it replaced the feather ball. It was made from the juice of the Palaquium genus of trees which was imported from South-East Asia. It arrived in bulk and full of impurities.

The gutty was easy to mass-produce – and it needed to be to meet demand. In 1897, it was estimated that 500 tons of gutta-percha was being used yearly for making balls.[1] This represents about 13,000,000 balls.

Coburn Haskell, inventor of the modern ball, was also a magnolia expert.

17

Walter Travis.

Demand was continually greater than supply as the game grew. In March 1899, Messrs J. & D. Clark of Musselburgh sold over 79,000 balls in one month, and had orders for 10 times that amount. By 1901, it was reckoned that there were over 20,000,000 gutty balls in use.

The rubber-cored ball was patented in the USA in 1898 by Coburn Haskell and Bertram Work, the latter an employee of the B.F. Goodrich Rubber Co. of Ohio. Two years later J. Gammeter, also of Goodrich, invented the first automatic golf-ball winding machine, which allowed the whole ball-making process to be mechanised.

In July 1901 reports of this new ball began to reach Britain. A small item in a report from the USA in *Golf Illustrated* mentioned a dispute over the use of the Haskell ball in a ladies' driving competition. Towards the end of September, reports recorded the sensation that the new ball had caused at the US Amateur Championship. Walter J. Travis won the qualifying medal using one, as did "all the western players". Travis went on to win the championship, defeating Walter Egan, who also used the new ball.

The first British opposition to the ball appeared in late October in the *Manchester Guardian*. The paper was hostile to the new ball, despite the fact that few people in Britain had actually seen one: "I really do not see why we should allow it [the Haskell] to come in. It should be slaughtered at the ports. The discovery of a ball that flies considerably further would be a menace to the game of golf. It would immediately make all our holes the wrong length."[2] Interestingly, this was to become the crux of the argument put forward by those who opposed the new ball.

In late October, the new ball may have reached St Andrews. John Low, a leading amateur golfer, claimed that he made the ball bounce the height of the R & A clubhouse, and that the next day he watched its owner, Mr Maitland, slice a tee shot with it. The ball supposedly landed on the steps of one of the houses on the Links and "bounded high in the air", never to be seen again. Horace Hutchinson, writing in 1919, told a different version of the same story, claiming that he sent the balls to Low to test. Low tested them indoors and lost a ball up a chimney. Hutchinson also claimed that he himself was the first man to play with the Haskell in Biarritz – something he never mentions in his various articles written in 1901 and 1902. In any event, the whole story sounds rather dubious and is not mentioned by either Low or Hutchinson in their copious writings over the next 18 months.

The ball arrived in Britain in meaningful quantities in November 1901. Messrs Spalding announced in the November 22nd *Golf Illustrated* that they had "just received a supply of the new Haskell golf balls from America". Harold Hilton and Horace Hutchinson reviewed the new ball in *The Sporting Chronicle* and *Country Life* respectively. Hilton did not find the Haskell "worth more in length than the ordinary gutty", but he did think that a short driver might get more distance. He also had trouble putting with it, because he could not "make it run with any uniformity". Like Hilton, Hutchinson did not find that it went any further off the tee, but it did go further when hit with an iron club and was a good ball for lofted

John Low.

approaches. He liked putting with it, but found it "very ill-suited for running up over rough ground".

Hutchinson was quite concerned about the quality and durability of the ball. He found that one in 12 balls was "distinctly inferior to the rest", and that up to four in 12 tended to crack easily. He concluded that "the best of them are very good balls and will last very much longer than a gutty if they are well treated", and that "the large percentage of indifferent balls makes the good ones turn out rather expensive" at 24 or 25 shillings (£1.20p or £1.25p) per dozen. The editor of *Golf Illustrated* was concerned by Hutchinson's remarks about the quality of the balls, and wrote on December 6th: "A ball that is going to knock out the 1 shilling (5p) gutty will have to be very much superior to that excellent article if it is to attract buyers at more than double the price." He reminded his readers that "when the gutty ball killed the old feather ball, it was not only an incomparably superior article, but it was sold at less than half the price."

As the year came to an end, John Low, who was to emerge as perhaps the foremost champion of the gutta ball, wrote: "The American ball has not revolutionised the game and the old gutta smiles again. The reason for this is that the ball has been tried and found wanting, not that the ball is too expensive . . . When our American friends send us over a ball that can be driven 50 yards further than the gutta, they will get plenty of half-crowns (12.5p) back in return."

What was actually becoming clear was that, while the new ball added appreciably to the distance of the long drivers, it was of greater help to those who were normally short off the tee. Of greater significance, it went much further when hit with an iron club. However, it was harder to control on and near the greens, requiring quite a different touch from the gutta ball. An American assessment of the new ball at the beginning of 1902 calculated that an amateur who hit a full drive 170 to 200 yards with the gutty would now hit a Haskell between 200 and 250 yards, and a brassie shot that formerly went 150-190 yards would now go 190-225 yards.[3] Iron shots could be hit 200 yards. On average the new ball went 30 to 50 yards further on full shots.

Undaunted, gutty manufacturers were continuing to bring out new styles. In the early months of 1902 the Pegasus, Agrippa and Argus all appeared. J.P. Cochrane and Co. announced that they were bringing out a new ball called the Rex, while Silvertown were introducing the Lynx. The golf ball market was large, healthy and highly competitive.

With all the publicity that the new ball had been receiving, it is not surprising that it quickly became very popular. *Golf Illustrated* reported in May 1902 that "quite a number of the best [amateur] players have taken to it."[4] There is no doubt that the Haskells were in short supply, but there is some doubt over the price being paid for them. Hutchinson, writing in 1919, said that "there was a time when as much as a guinea [£1.05p] apiece was paid for them, and numbers changed hands at 10 shillings [50p]." Darwin, writing in 1952, said that he tried to buy some before the 1902 Amateur Championship "but no more were to be had for love or money". John

Charles Hutchings, 1903.

Low, writing in 1903, said "they could hardly be bought except for gold". Yet in the many articles and newspaper reports written over the period under discussion, there is much criticism of the price of the new ball, because of the price of 2 shillings (10p) or 3 shillings (15p) a ball, compared to 1 shilling (5p) for a gutty. There are occasional references to higher prices being paid, but this was never an issue.

The situation seems to have been as follows. The manufacturer's retail price for a Haskell was 2 shillings (10p) and, later, the Kempshall was 3 shillings (15p). This is clearly stated in all the advertisements and in all the references in the pages of *Golf Illustrated* and the other papers and journals. It was the club professionals and some retailers who were charging the very high prices for the ball, as stated in the November 7th, 1902 *Golf Illustrated*: "The few professionals who secured themselves some have usually asked exorbitant prices for them." The result of this was that "their club members have gone to [the manufacturers'] headquarters where they could buy at a lower price." *Golf Illustrated* mentions 10 shillings (50p) being charged for a ball in the November 21st, 1902 issue. There were constant supply problems throughout 1902, but there can be little doubt that when the rubber-cored balls were available, they could be purchased at normal price from the majority of suppliers and, in the minority of cases, at inflated prices at some club professionals' shops and other outlets.

The first major tournament success by a player using the new ball in Britain was at the 1902 Amateur Championship, played from April 29th to

Robert Maxwell, *c.* **1910.**

May 1st. Both Charles Hutchings, the winner, and Sidney Fry, the losing finalist, used Haskells. Robert Maxwell, John Ball and Edward Blackwell were all using the new ball at around the time of the Championship, but it is not clear if any of them used it in the tournament itself. Certainly the new rubber-cored ball was so widely used in the Championship that none could be had for the next fortnight.

In the week after the Amateur Championship came the R & A May Meeting, and it was reported that "many of the leading players, including Mr Blackwell the medallist, used them [rubber-cored balls] in the medal competition."[5] During the week, there had been a great run on the Haskell and the local ball makers were "quite sold out". The next week, in the Royal Liverpool Spring Medal, John Graham used a gutty, John Ball used

Edward Blackwell.

John Graham in foul weather.

both types of ball and "with regard to the handicap results, the majority of the winners made use of the American invention with very satisfactory results."[6]

The new ball was widely used at the Ladies' Amateur Championship from May 27th to May 30th, 1902, where it was reported in *Golf Illustrated* that "seldom has there been more brilliancy shown on the greens and in the majority of instances the ball was a Haskell." Both the finalists, Miss Hezlet and Miss Nevile, used the rubber-cored ball.

Thus there can be no doubt that the new ball was being widely used within the amateur game, whenever it was available. However, the professionals took a different view. The editor of *Golf Illustrated* asked the leading British professionals for their opinion of the new ball. James Braid wrote: "I found very little difference in the length of drive between them and gutta balls; perhaps they run further, but certainly don't carry as far . . . They are also more difficult to stop when approaching and on the putting green are very liable to jump out of the hole." Sandy Herd found the Haskell difficult to putt with, "it hasn't got the click to guide you on the putting greens such as the gutta ball has. What one thinks he can gain on the drive, he will very soon lose on the putting green." Neither Vardon nor Taylor liked the ball. On the other hand, Andrew Kirkaldy liked the ball, saying "There's no muckle wrong wi't."[7]

Sandy Herd won the Open Championship played on June 4th and 5th using the Haskell, and Harry Vardon may well have lost because his partner used this ball. Both these statements require some detailed explanation. It is apparent that Herd had not really tested the Haskell when he wrote his letter to *Golf Illustrated*. When he arrived at Hoylake, Herd arranged for a practice round with John Ball. Herd said in his autobiography in 1923 "He [Ball] was using the Haskell ball and doing such wonders with it that I found myself envying him. I had not seen the rubber-cored ball before, and when we reached the 15th hole, Mr Ball, smiling at my comments regarding his drives, gave me a Haskell to try. That was the end of the gutty ball

Alex Herd.

for me . . . What impressed me chiefly was that the Haskell could be driven without effort." Herd then went to Jack Morris's shop, where he was able to purchase four balls. The account in *Golf Illustrated* on June 13th is slightly different. It was reported that Herd used the Haskell "although not exclusively in the actual championship" and his conversion to the ball "was only partial".

Bernard Darwin, in his biography of James Braid, wrote that Herd "alone of the leading professionals had used the Haskell". At least one lesser professional, Peter McEwan, used the new ball – much to the detriment of Harry Vardon. Vardon was the leader after two rounds, and was drawn to play the third round with McEwan. Vardon, despite using a gutty, still constantly outdrove McEwan, who usually ended up playing his approach shot first. Vardon watched him pitch the Haskell short of the green and then ran up onto it. He constantly told himself not to take any notice, "but as every golfer knows, the inclination to judge the run by that which the other player obtains is irresistible." He tried to pitch "farther and farther to allow for the difference between the rubber core and the gutty but something . . . seemed to hold me back and I was always short."[8] In the end, Vardon lost the Championship by a single stroke.

The new ball's greatest assets were that it required less physical force to produce a given result, and that it generally went further. This made it very popular with most average golfers. As was remarked in *Golf Illustrated*: "I feel certain that no power on earth, except perhaps the police, will deter men from using a ball that will add to the length of their drive."[9]

Not everybody was enamoured with the new ball, despite, or because of, its success to date. The traditionalists, led by John Low, felt that it threatened the purity of the game. In fact the traditionalists came to espouse a radical cause, namely that of seeking a standard ball for the game – as long as it was the gutta ball.

In July 1902 John Low wrote a long attack on the new ball in *Athletic News*. His main criticism was that the new ball gave an unfair advantage to weak drivers, who on two-shot holes (par 4s), would now be able to reach the green and thereby have a chance to defeat the better player. He argued that the best golf links were laid out to test the power of players using the gutta-percha ball, and "at present in this gutta age, the long driver, if he be also straight, derives a certain and fixed advantage on good courses from his power of play." To him "golf must continue to be a game in which strength and power play a certain part." While denying he was advocating a standard ball, he argued a good case for one.

The weakness of his arguments was exposed in *Golf Illustrated* on July 18th and 25th. It was rightly pointed out that more than pure power was needed to play most holes. In any event, if changes needed to be introduced to make holes more challenging, "golf courses will have to be altered to suit . . . just as the present courses have been altered since the gutta percha ball arrived." It was also pointed out that rubber-cored balls went further, but were not easier to hit accurately.

An article in August 1902 in *The Field* thought that the new balls were too expensive. The correspondent in *Golf Illustrated* thought that the price would soon fall, and that they represented good value in real terms. They lasted six times longer than gutties and were less severe on wooden clubs. Even at three times the price of a gutty, they were good value.

It was now apparent that there were two lines of argument against the new ball – it was too expensive, and it might ruin the layout of golf courses. This second point raised the issue of whether there should be a standard ball. *Golf Illustrated* opposed a standard ball because the new ball introduced a new element of skill in the short game; good players would still defeat lesser players and to do so "would lead to the establishment of a similar standard in regard to clubs and that would destroy much of the essential interest and charm of the game".[10]

In September 1902, Low and Mure Fergusson brought the issue to the R & A Rules of Golf Committee, of which they were both members. The R & A was the ruling body of the game, and in the end the golfing world looked to it to settle the issue. At the meeting on September 22nd, Mure Fergusson moved "That the new rubber filled balls are calculated to spoil the game of golf as now played over links laid out for the gutta percha ball and that it would be advisable to bring in a new rule for the regulation of balls and clubs to be used in playing the game." The motion was seconded by John Low. Mr Hall Blyth introduced an amendment saying that the committee was not yet in a position to bring forward any recommendation on the subject. It was defeated by seven votes to five, and Mure Fergusson's motion was carried by the same margin. He was instructed to draft a motion "for consideration of the Rules of Golf Committee and thereafter, if approved by them, to be submitted to the General Meeting of the Club in May". Low and Mure Fergusson had won a small victory and, although there were two major hurdles still to come, there was a chance that the gutta ball could become the standard ball.

Low went on the offensive. In *Athletic News*, Low returned to his theme of courses being ruined by the new ball and wrote, "St Andrews has now become an ideal course for the second-rate player . . . Formerly the greens could only be conquered by long driving, but now the holes are within the compass of infirm old gentlemen."[11] This was countered by Hall Blyth, who was chairman of the Rules of Golf Committee and was publicly backing the new ball. He "frankly confessed to liking them not only because they improved his game materially, but also because playing with them was pleasant".[12]

On October 6th, Low wrote another piece in *Athletic News,* once again arguing that the great danger of the rubber-cored ball was that it would ruin the existing golf courses. Horace Hutchinson wrote a swift and effective rebuttal to Low in *Golf Illustrated* on October 17th. He was firmly against any type of standardisation, and felt that "those who make the most noise do so because they are annoyed to find men whom they could beat with the gutty coming up to an equality to them with the Haskell." He concluded by stating that "the best merit of the Haskell ball and the reason it will prevail . . . is that it makes the game much more pleasant to play because it leaves the club so easily . . . For after all, we do pretend and assume that we play the game for pleasure." The opponents of the new ball in the autumn of 1902 were a few of the leading amateurs and most of the professionals. These were all men who had thoroughly mastered the gutta ball, and they were widely seen by contemporaries as trying to protect their position within the game.

As was aptly pointed out in an article "The Humours of the New Ball" in *Golf Illustrated* on October 31st, "The novice . . . hears that the Haskell improves an indifferent player's game . . . He invests in a Haskell [imagining] that he is by mere possession of that ball, half way on the road to becoming a Hilton or a Herd. After a considerable time it dawns on his intelligence that the circumference of a Haskell is no greater than that of the gutty, and that, therefore, the chances of missing or topping the balls are equal."

Meanwhile, possibly in an attempt to draw the debate over the new ball to an end, the editor of *Golf Illustrated* took the unprecedented step of writing to the prime minister, A.J. Balfour, asking for his opinion on the issue. Balfour, the great golfing enthusiast, replied on October 31st: "Sir, those who fear that any considerable improvement in golf balls will necessitate a corresponding modification in the length of our courses, have much to say for themselves. But I should view with great apprehension the introduction into golf of so great a novelty as that of the standardisation of the implements to be used by the player. Such standardisation cannot logically be restricted to the balls, and it would be a pity, I think to destroy the practically unlimited freedom of selection which among all games, belongs, so far as I know, alone to golf." Such a firm declaration by the prime minister should have settled the debate. It didn't.

The next opposition came from the professionals, who did not like the new ball for purely economic reasons. As will be seen, ball and club sales were an important part of the club professionals' income. They made less of a mark-up on the new balls, and they could not make the balls. They were losing sales of other golfing equipment when customers bought their balls direct from the suppliers, and the new balls broke fewer wooden clubs than the gutties.

On November 14th, 1902 the secretary of the fledgling Professional Golfers' Association wrote to the secretary of the Open Championship Committee asking that only the gutty ball be allowed at the Open. The reasoning was in line with Low's arguments, namely that the new ball was "not conducive to the advancement of golf as a game of skill", and "the championship courses afford ample scope for the player's skill without the aid of the mechanical advantage which the rubber cored ball affords."

The Prestwick club passed the matter back to the R & A, whose deliberations were expected in May.

The PGA then took a different approach, and at their AGM on December 8th passed a motion "That for the present, only gutty balls be used in tournaments promoted by the Association." This caused a fresh outcry, more controversy and a good deal of criticism of the professionals. The editor of *Golf Illustrated* wrote on December 12th, "I am only expressing the opinion which I have heard on all hands when I say the professionals' action is both useless for the object which they desire and most ill-advised for their own interests." Most other press reports were critical of the PGA.

The beginning of the end of the whole debate happened very quickly over a three month period beginning in March 1903. On March 25th and 26th, a tournament was held in Bournemouth, in which Herd, White, Braid and Taylor played. Taylor, one of the founders of the PGA, used a rubber-cored ball, as the account of the match in *Golf Illustrated* clearly states that Braid "was the only player to use the gutty ball".

The next day, the Rules of Golf Committee met to consider the rubber-

Jack White, 1904 Open champion.

cored ball. As requested at the previous meeting, Mure Fergusson put forward his motion: "That in the opinion of the Rules of Golf Committee, legislation has become necessary to deal with the new conditions caused by the introduction of the rubber-cored ball and other inventions. They therefore ask this Meeting to empower the Committee to draw up regulations . . . with a view to preserving the high standard of the game of golf as a trial of strength as well as skill. They would further suggest that the Royal and Ancient Golf Club should advise the other Clubs connected with the Open and Amateur Championships that they are in favour of having these competitions decided by the use of the gutta ball, pending the framing of the aforementioned regulations."

The motion was defeated by ten votes to five. Thus the Rules of Golf Committee effectively settled the issue by voting to take no action. It was up to individuals to choose which ball they wished to play with. This decision became public knowledge at the end of April.

On May 15th, Braid and Vardon were both reported using the new ball. They claimed they were doing so as a result of the decision of the Rules of Golf Committee not to legislate against the new ball. At the Open Championship on June 10th and 11th, Vardon won using a Haskell, as did the other top five finishers, Tom Vardon, Jack White, Sandy Herd and James Braid. An advertisement for Haskell balls noted the top five finishers and then simply said "Comment Unnecessary."

The gutta ball did not disappear overnight. However, by July 1905, the Agrippa Company had a massive clearance sale of all their gutty balls. In November of the same year, *Golf Illustrated* reported that R. Forgan and Son were making a collection of the "now almost extinct gutta ball" and had collected almost 100 varieties.

As late as April 1914 an exhibition match using the gutty ball and featuring Vardon, Braid, Taylor and George Duncan was held at Sandy Lodge Golf Club. After the match, it was reported in *Golf Illustrated* that the gutty ball had passed away forever. At the end of the day, the game of golf as played with the rubber-cored ball was much simpler and more enjoyable than it ever had been with the gutty ball. In an editorial written before that match Harold Hilton reminded his readers that the "present popularity of golf is undoubtedly due to the resilient ball; one cannot get away from that fact."

This assertion is borne out by the evidence. As pointed out previously, there was a lull in new club foundations between 1897 and 1902, and especially in new clubs with courses. There could be several explanations for this. The first might be that the first generation of enthusiasts had reached its peak and the dramatic upturn after 1902 could be attributed to a new wave of players coming of age. The second could be the economic and social impact of the Boer War, which would explain the downturn between 1899 and 1901. The third could be the effect of the new ball. In all probability it was a combination of all three factors. However the revival after 1902 coincides so closely with the acceptance of the rubber-cored ball that, taken together with Hilton's assertion, the indications are that the new ball had a major impact on the growth of the game. There were 1,503 clubs at the end of 1902 and eight years later this total had risen to 2,729. Clubs with their own course grew from 1,010 in 1902 to 1,699 by 1910.

The drop in the professionals' income from ball sales and repairs, as a result of the rubber-cored ball replacing the gutty, was to remain an issue up to 1914. Although the professionals did not see it that way, they benefited in the long term. They gained more customers, especially ladies, and more jobs at club level were created. In turn, the increased popularity at club level led to more professional tournaments and exhibitions.

The loss of some clubs

Ironically the motion presented to the Rules of Golf Committee to attempt to ban the rubber-cored ball led directly to another major equipment controversy – the first restrictions on the form and make of golf clubs. Mure Fergusson's motion called not only for regulation of the ball but also of clubs. The concept of regulation of clubs came to the fore as part of the Rules of Golf revision that began in 1907. The new rules, which came into effect in 1909, contained an "intimation" that stated: "The Rules of Golf Committee intimates that it will not sanction any substantial departure from the traditional and accepted form and make of golf clubs, which in its opinion consists of a plain shaft and a head which contains no mechanical contrivance such as springs."

This intimation was in direct response to the number of unusual clubs which were coming on to the market, as indeed was the rule change of 1910. Neither was aimed at specifically barring the Schenectady putter, which Walter Travis used to win the 1904 Amateur Championship.

There was no controversy over the 1909 intimation. However, this was not the case with the next foray of the Rules of Golf Committee into the form and make of clubs.

On August 13th, 1909 *Golf Illustrated* ran its monthly feature on the "Decisions of the Rules of Golf Committee". One of the August decisions was in response to a question submitted by the Nga Motu Golf Club in New Zealand: "With regard to 'Make and Form of Golf Clubs', is it permissible to use a small croquet mallet to putt with?" To which the decision was "A croquet mallet is not a golf club, and is inadmissible." For the next 14 months, until October 1910, there was great confusion and controversy as to what was, and was not, an acceptable golf club.

Nobody seemed quite sure of the full ramifications of this decision. Did it mean simply what it said? Did it apply to all mallet-headed clubs? Did it apply to other types of clubs? There was much speculation in the pages of *Golf Illustrated* about what this all meant, but the Rules of Golf Committee remained officially silent. However, by November 1909, it seemed to have become common knowledge that the decision by the committee would include the banning of all centre-shafted clubs. Garden Smith, the editor of *Golf Illustrated*, came out very strongly against this, writing on November 12th: "The mallet-headed or centre-shafted club cannot by any stretch of imagination be regarded as a menace to the game. So far as we are aware,

James Braid.

they are not used by any of the professionals and by very few, if any, of the leading amateurs . . . The Rules of Golf Committee might have been better advised to allow these mallet-headed and centre-shafted clubs to die a natural death and reserve their energies to suppress any invention, either in club or ball, whether by mechanical device or otherwise, that would make the game easier."

Whereas Smith shied away from the question of the need to define what was a legal club, J.H. Taylor took the opposite view, writing in the next issue: "The standardisation of golf clubs may be a difficult matter to tackle, and the definition of what should constitute a golf club still more so; yet I think the time is come when this question should be forced to the very front of the golfer's politics."

As the Spring Meeting of the R & A approached, the documented intentions of the Rules of Golf Committee became clearer, with discussions on the drafting of new rule. Then at the May Meeting itself, Captain Burn, the committee chairman, explained to the club members that it was the object of the Rules of Golf Committee to maintain the old shape of the golf club as nearly as possible, and that, therefore, they were prepared to object to any clubs substantially differing therefrom. All centre-headed clubs, including the Schenectady putter, would be ruled as inadmissible. Also inadmissible were iron clubs, which, by a bend in the neck, could be made identical with an ordinary mallet club; in other words, any club whose shaft would pass through the centre of the face. Captain Burn explained that the mallet-type club was one in which the head was not all on one side of the shaft.

This explanation brought the confusion and controversy to new heights. However no new rules had been passed. The Rules of Golf Committee had been empowered to make the changes, but the changes, and a precise definition, had not yet occurred. Over the summer while all the controversy raged, including with the USGA, the committee worked on the wording of the new rule, which was then passed at the R & A Autumn Meeting. The final wording was much clearer than the statements made in May, and carefully defined what constituted a mallet head, a centre shaft or a wry neck.

The only real problem that this new rule gave to professionals was how to dispose of their stock of now-banned clubs. As Garden Smith had said, very few of them ever used these types of clubs. It had no bearing on how they played, it just meant that they might have had a smaller range of clubs to sell in their shops.

NOTES

1. *Golf*, December 10th, 1897
2. *Golf Illustrated*, October 25th, 1901
3. *Golf Illustrated*, January 24th, 1902
4. *Golf Illustrated*, May 9th, 1902
5. *Golf Illustrated*, May 16th, 1902
6. *Golf Illustrated*, May 23rd, 1902
7. *Golf Illustrated*, May 23rd and June 6th, 1902
8. *How to Play Golf*, Harry Vardon, 1912
9. *Golf Illustrated*, July 4th, 1902
10. *Golf Illustrated*, August 29th, 1902
11. Quoted in *Golf Illustrated*, October 3rd, 1902
12. *Golf Illustrated*, October 3rd, 1902

2. The Birth of the PGA

LATE NINETEENTH CENTURY BRITISH CLASS DISTINCTIONS carried over into sports. Cricket provided the prime example of the distinction between gentlemen and players. The two groups ate separately, changed separately, travelled separately and came on to the field through different entrances. Such distinctions were equally visible in golf. Professional players did not use the club house, and the social chasm between them and the club members was recognised and was not to be crossed.

In crude terms, the professionals came from working class or artisan backgrounds: Braid was a joiner by trade; Herd was a journeyman baker and plasterer; Vardon and Taylor both worked as gardeners as youths. Golf was seen as a way of advancement. The status of a golf professional had risen from the rather bleak prospects outlined by Hutchinson in 1890 to the point where, under the 1907 Workmen's Compensation Act, they were bracketed with governesses, curates, pew-openers and jockeys.

The leading professionals could command reasonable terms for themselves. Under the terms of his 1917 contract at Walton Heath, James Braid was paid £100 per year, quarterly, and could charge 37.5p per round to play with members and 25p per hour for lessons. He could be away from the club for 90 days of the year – but no more than 14 days at a time, except for important competitions and tournaments. He did, however, have to supply his own replacement. He ran the shop, and was allowed to sell clubs to non-members and to design golf courses. Yet, on the other hand, Andrew Kirkaldy was receiving a wage of only £1 a week, with a fee of 12.5p per round, when he became the Professional to the R & A in 1910.

Open winners could expect additional rewards from their home club. For example, Harry Vardon received a "purse of sovereigns" from Ganton after his 1896 win, and Braid's presentations from Walton Heath escalated over time. In 1908, he received £140 and, in 1910, £200.

It was not unusual for a popular professional to receive a testimonial when he left his club. Tom Vardon was given £50 by Ilkley Golf Club, while his successor, Douglas McEwan, was given £53 by Musselburgh Golf Club. On the occasion of his marriage, George Duncan received a clock and side ornaments, and a cheque for an unspecified amount, from the

Tom Vardon, with James Braid to his right.

members of his club at Timperley.

At the turn of the century, it was estimated that an unskilled town or agricultural labourer earned approximately £95 per annum. An established county cricket player earned about £275 for a five-month season, from which he had to deduct the cost of his own equipment and of travel to away matches. He therefore netted something in the region of £120 to £150 per year. A test player might net as much as £200. Cricketers also had the possibility of winter tours and benefits to add to their earnings. In 1908 the Football Association imposed a maximum wage of £4 on players in England. This put a theoretical ceiling of £208 a year on their earnings. However, players often earned more through bonuses, international match fees and so on. There was no maximum wage limit in Scottish football, but the best players still earned a basic wage of no more than £4 a week. By 1900 Rugby League players were earning between £1.50 and £4 a week.

Advantages of the professional

Golfers had three advantages over the professionals in cricket, football and rugby. Professional golfers had no restraints on their moving from one appointment to another compared to the two-year qualification rule in cricket and the retain and transfer system in football. The second advantage was that their basic earnings were club-based rather than match-based. This meant that they enjoyed far longer careers than those who earned money only in their peak competitive years. Thirdly, for a limited number of professional golfers, another source of income was golf course design.

'Old' Tom Morris.

In his later years, Tom Morris Senior was a prolific course designer, while Willie Park Junior was probably the most gifted golf course architect amongst his contemporaries. He quickly concentrated his abilities on course design and club manuafacture more than tournament and exhibition play. James Braid became perhaps the most prolific course designer, largely after World War I, and J.H. Taylor and Harry Vardon were also involved in the design of many courses in Britain and Europe. However, with the exception of Park, most viewed golf course architecture as only an addition to their club duties.

The average professional golfers were neither better off, nor worse off, than their peers in other sports or trades. They were not particularly well paid, and the delicate balance between their salary, their teaching fees and the income from the making and selling of clubs and balls was a constant source of controversy. Problems with the last part of the equation led directly to the foundation of the Professional Golfers' Association.

Willie Park Junior, c. 1920.

Professionals in a tournament organised by Lord Dudley at Witley Court in this period. They are, from left to right: J.H. Taylor, Harry Vardon, Ben Sayers, Willie Auchterlonie, Andrew Kirkaldy, Willie Fernie, James Braid, George Cawsey, Alex Herd and Jack White.

Throughout this period, golf as a game was run by amateurs for amateurs, many of whom in turn viewed professionals in the paternalistic manner that was so typical of the period. John Low, for instance, wrote in 1899 that: "Golf may well be proud of its present professional players, and they are well worthy of the support that they receive from the amateur world."[1]

Amateur *versus* professional

Eight years later, Horace Hutchinson was concerned over the relationship between amateurs and professionals, and wrote: "Those of the professional class itself, who are the most level-headed and clear sighted, are the very first to see and to say that the professional has, for the present, gone far enough; that it is a mistake for the amateur to lift him right out of his place and exalt him, as a schoolboy is apt to exalt his athletic instructor."[2]

Later that same year, an article in *Golf Illustrated* declared: "We admire the independent spirit of the professionals and do not doubt their ability to manage their own affairs, but it is well to recognise that the professionals cannot become an independent body without serious danger to existing relations. The less the professional needs the amateur, the less interest will the amateur take in him."[3]

A *Golf Illustrated* editorial on January 28th, 1910 that announced that the journal was now an "official organ" of the PGA, stated: "They [the professionals] will still further the sympathy and good understanding that already happily exists between them and their amateur patrons." The clubs did act as patrons. They often paid for their professional to enter the Open and for their expenses, in return, as the writer in 1895 put it, "for having the honour of their employers to maintain".[4]

The professionals, like their counterparts in cricket and other sports, had no option but to accept the status quo. Major changes could come only from corresponding changes in society. These derived from the effects of World War I.

Players were able, however, to mix with their betters, strictly on the

Freddie Tait, Amateur champion, 1896.

latters' terms. The cream of society liked to employ their own personal golf professionals from time to time, either for a season, or for a few days or weeks. *Golf Illustrated* reported in 1903 that: "a professional golfer has now become as necessary an adjunct to all the great country houses as the gamekeeper. The Duke of Devonshire has two professionals, and so has Lord Londonderry, Mr Leopold Rothschild, Mr Percy Wyndham, and nearly all the country gentlemen who have courses on their own grounds, have professional players for the use and assistance of their guests."[5]

It was not uncommon for even the leading players to be at the beck and call of the great men of the land. For example, Taylor and Vardon spent time with Viscount Curzon in 1899; Ben Sayers was one of the Duke of Devonshire's two professionals at the turn of the century; Willie Auchterlonie went to Ireland in 1904 to coach the Earl of Dudley and Willie Fernie spent two months with the Duke of Portland at Welbeck Abbey in 1906.

Although the amateur was the professional's social superior, unlike in cricket, he was not his golfing superior. Although amateurs had been competing in the Open since 1861, John Ball was the first to win it, in 1890. Harold Hilton won in 1892, and then again in 1897, on his home course at Hoylake. After that, until 1914, the closest any amateur came was Hilton again, in 1911, when he finished third, but only one stroke back. Hilton and Robert Maxwell each finished two strokes behind in 1898 and 1902 respectively. The worst year for amateurs was 1905, when none played in the final round. Between 1894 and 1914, no amateur was in serious contention for the title in 15 Opens.

The best amateurs did not fare very well in head-to-head competitions against the leading professionals in the two major team matches in 1894 and 1911. In the Gentlemen *v* Players Match in 1894, Hilton, A.D. Blyth, Charles Hutchings, Mure Fergusson, Horace Hutchinson and Alexander Stuart all lost to their professional opponent in the first round. Only Ball and Tait won their matches, but Ball lost in the next round and Tait in the semifinal. In the Coronation Match played in 1911, which consisted of nine foursomes matches, only one amateur team, L.O. Munn and H.W. Beveridge, took a point, and their match against Rowland Jones and Michael Moran went to the 38th hole. The professionals won the rest of the matches handily, and the whole event was described as "an amateur Waterloo".

"Simpler quieter lives"
Both the amateurs and the professionals were aware of the competitive gap that had opened up. F. Kinloch, writing in 1908, ascribed the difference in their games to the constant practice of both the game and of playing in front of large crowds that the professionals had. He also felt that the social divide made a difference: "They [the professionals] lead simpler, quieter lives, eating less and drinking less, going to bed earlier and rising earlier; moreover, they have fewer business worries, and are thus able to concentrate all their energies, mental as well as physical on the game."[6] It is unlikely that many professionals would have agreed with this analysis, especially with regard to not having money worries and the virtue of being able to afford less to eat! A year later, J.H. Taylor attributed the difference to the fact that professionals tended to start life as caddies, and that a caddie "learns the game in its absolute entirety", while "the amateur learns his game in a superficial manner."[7]

A week later, Harold Hilton gave his views. He felt that Taylor had not gone sufficiently deeply into the issues. He argued that a man's golfing education did not "begin and end in the days of early youth". The advantage that the professional had was that, as his livelihood depended on the game,

Rowland Jones.

he had constantly to "think everything out, particularly in relation to his own game. He knows his own game, its strengths and its weaknesses, and had invariably some antidote for his shortcomings." In other words, it came down to constant practice towards a final purpose. He felt that an amateur could do this: "if only he took the trouble to do so – but it rather suggests making a labour of the game – and the majority cannot see why they should do so." The amateur "is content to obtain as much amusement and pleasure as he can out of the game and leave the hard labour alone".

It is interesting to note that Hilton's argument went totally against the ethos of how amateurs were supposed to play cricket. A gentleman batsman was expected to turn out for his county when time permitted, and score heavily, regardless of how short of match practice he might be.

The telling factor against the leading amateurs was undoubtedly the lack of constant practice, and the lack of match practice against the top professionals. Aside from very occasional exhibition matches, the Open Championship was the only time that both types of player met regularly, and that was only once a year.

In 1901 it was reckoned in an article in *Tit Bits* that a professional golfer had five potential sources of income. He received a basic salary from his club of up to £1 per week and, usually, also received fees for teaching of about 17.5p per round, or 10p per hour. He was expected to make and repair clubs and also sell balls, which could net him between £70 and £150 per year. The last two sources – playing in tournaments and exhibition matches – were usually only available to the leading players. It was estimated that the top professionals could earn between £300 and £400 a year, but the majority were earning considerably less. Only a few professionals at this time could count on fees from course design. A "Southern Pro", writing to *Golf Illustrated* in 1901, pointed out that many clubs paid between 50p and 75p per week, and that he himself earned the latter. He made 12.5p per round, and had an average of only two rounds per week.[8] Arthur Ryle, in 1910, reminded everyone that out of the basic salary of £1, a professional would need to pay an assistant from his own pocket to help run the shop while the professional was out on the course. He estimated that cost to be between 75p and 90p per week, and thus the professionals' real earnings were considerably less than was believed.[9]

Club-making and income

In the spring of 1901, the professionals were much agitated by the growing practice by golf clubs of selling the club- and ball-making business to the highest bidder, thus depriving the resident professional of an important part of his annual income. Other clubs were turning the situation on its head, and cutting the professional's salary if it was felt he was "making a good thing out of club making".

Taylor wrote to *Golf Illustrated* on March 29th, praising the journal for taking a stand against this practice, which, he felt, if continued, would return the professional to "the state of comparative poverty common not a great many years ago". Harry Vardon wrote the following week endorsing Taylor's views. He added that were his own club not "one of the best", he would have returned permanently to the USA.

On April 12th, letters by White, Braid, Herd and C.S. Butchart all appeared in *Golf Illustrated*. White wrote; "The practice of letting the club-making business of a club to the highest bidder is another thing that is doing a lot of injury to professional golf. I consider that first class professional golfers (and there are a lot of good men today) are very much underpaid. Why shouldn't good, steady men, when in their prime, have the opportunity to lay away enough for a rainy day?." Braid felt that the cutting of salaries, if the club thought the professional was making too much from his shop, could not be condemned too strongly. Herd supported Taylor and Vardon. Butchart felt "it will be a pity, through the shortsightedness of the clubs themselves, that by driving the professionals out of the market [of clubs and balls] they will reduce the status of golf, both as a profession and game." A letter appearing in the same issue and signed by "A Professional in North Wales" went one step further than those written by the above, and suggested that "the time is now ripe for the professionals to band themselves into an association to promote the general welfare of the professionals and look after their interests." He expressed the hope that this idea would be taken up by the leading professionals.

The following week, April 19th, this idea was taken one step further by "A North of England Professional". He said that he was surprised that only the North Wales Professional had suggested a remedy to better the lot of the poor professional: "Of course men like Taylor, Braid, Vardon, Herd, Jack White etc., seeing they can practically command their own terms, cannot be included in the class 'poor professional' . . . but unless the initiative be taken by some of those leading men, any attempt to ameliorate the condition of the poor professional is doomed to failure". He challenged Taylor, "if he is really in earnest" to take "this matter up and I am sure he will have the hearty co-operation and earn the deep gratitude of all connected with our noble profession".

In that same issue an editorial warned: "It will be a bad day for golf in this country, if by niggardly or inconsiderate treatment, our best players are driven from our shores." The next week, April 26th, the "Professional in North Wales" urged Taylor to "come forward at our call for help to formulate some scheme for the better treatment of our poor and downtrodden brothers." He warned "we must have some organisation or there will be worse things to come, even for the fortunate ones."

A professional association
Taylor did indeed take up the challenge. It is ironic that, although the first public suggestions for the formation of an association came from professionals in Wales and Northern England, the organisation formed was the "London and Counties Golf Professionals Association", serving members in south-east England. The first meeting of the new association mentioned in *Golf Illustrated* was held on September 9th, 1901, when Taylor was elected chairman, and Braid elected captain. Its aims were to assist professional golfers with an employment agency, a benevolent fund and the holding of competitions. At its first Annual General Meeting, held on December 2nd, 1901, the name was changed to the less cumbersome "Professional Golfers' Association", and its membership was extended to all professional golfers, club makers and their assistants in the United Kingdom.

In early 1902, the "Northern Counties Professional Golfers Association" was formed with 30 members, and with Harry Vardon acting as chairman. At a meeting on February 27th, 1902, the Northern Association declined an invitation to amalgamate with the PGA, but a month later on March 24th, it changed its mind and became part of the PGA, as did the Midland Golf Association.

The PGA was not the first body to attempt to "do something" for the professionals. *Golf Illustrated* had set up a Golf Employment Bureau in 1898, but it seems not to have amounted to very much. The magazine also set up a "Golfers Fund for the Widows and Orphans of those who fall in the Transvaal War" in 1899, a fund that included a "Golf Professionals' War Fund". The Midland Golf Association had been set up in 1897 "to link the professionals together for common purposes – indeed a kind of professional golf trade union".[10] In early 1899, the Midland Golf Association opened its ranks to professionals outside the area, and sent a circular inviting other regions to set up similar associations. It was a direct forerunner of, and then part of, the PGA.

As will be seen, the formation of the PGA was to change the function and structure of tournament golf in Britain, but its primary objective was to look after the welfare of professional golfers. To this end it set up a benevolent fund, to which among the first contributors were the proprietors of *Golf Illustrated*. Charles Mieville became the honorary secretary in February 1902, replacing Frank Johnson, who had acted as secretary *pro tem*. By March, Mieville had the PGA Employment Agency in full working order, and had already "effected some satisfactory engagements".

The benevolent fund
Much effort went into soliciting money for the Benevolent Fund. The objects of the fund were to relieve deserving members of the association by temporary or permanent grants; by assisting in pressing cases to prevent the lapsing of life, accident or other policies; by assisting in cases of sickness, accident or death; by providing small annuities to the aged and incapacitated; and by making allowances to widows and orphans. One of the more interesting fund-raising events was a cricket match played at Lords on August 31st, 1903, in which a team of Cricket-Golfers lost to the Golf-Cricketers. In the best amateur tradition, Lt C. Hutchison and Jack Graham opened for the Golfers and scored 60 and 29, laying the foundation of a last-wicket victory. Taylor scored 12, Braid 7, White 7 and Herd was out for a duck. Later that same year, a concert was held at the Queen's Hall, London, also to raise money.

By the year ending March 31st, 1905, the Benevolent Fund stood at £426.42p, but, because of pressures of the expansion of the game and the growth in members, the fund had decreased to £71.50p by 1910. Another round of urgent appeals for funds was launched with some success.

The problems about lost income from ball sales that had provided some of the motivation for forming the PGA surfaced again almost immediately, with the advent of the rubber-cored ball. As already mentioned, the PGA opposed the new ball. This public opposition from the infant organisation created a great deal of criticism. *Golf Illustrated* turned on the PGA, and an article on December 12th, 1902 said: "The Professionals' Association is largely benevolent in its objects and depends almost entirely for its welfare on the good offices of amateur golfers and clubs, and at its formation, I repeatedly warned its members of the false position they would place their society in if at any time they allowed it to assume political functions and attempted to run independently of, or in opposition to, the great body of amateurs". A week later, the PGA was accused of having a swelled head as a result of its immediate success. *The Pall Mall* felt that "the professionals have made a big tactical mistake." *The Scotsman* was surprised that an intelligent body of men such as the PGA "lent themselves to this policy of boycotting". *The Manchester Courier* thought that the PGA was alienating the sympathy of the majority of amateurs, and that their boycott was ill-advised. In fact the boycott never came about, and the controversy died. The whole tone of the criticism of the PGA forcibly showed the status of professionals in relation to amateurs: the professionals' opinions could be sought by the amateurs, but they were not in a position to make demands.

The issue came alive again in 1907, when some professionals were criticised for entering into an agreement with an American manufacturer to push its balls in consideration of better terms. *The Daily Chronicle* argued that this would hurt the British ball industry and was against the interests of amateur players. Garden Smith, in *Golf Illustrated* on May 3rd, disagreed with this and declared that "the professionals' actions in this is, in our opinion, in no way detrimental to the amateurs' interest, nor in any way an abuse of their position as 'paid servants' of amateur clubs." He did think, however, that it would have been better for the PGA to have sought better terms from British manufacturers before having taken this course of action.

Selling balls

Again the storm passed, only for the fundamental issue of who controlled the pro shop to come up again in January 1910. A new club advertised for a professional, but the terms stated that the club intended to reserve for itself the right of selling balls to its members. Taylor wrote to *Golf Illustrated* on January 21st, pointing out that the "right of selling balls to the members has always been recognised as the sole prerogative of the professional attached to the club from the earliest days of the game". He reiterated how the re-making of balls "which I venture to say was his [the professional's] chief source of income" was swept away by the advent of the rubber-cored ball. He accepted that they now made a higher profit on balls, but actually sold fewer, because the rubber-cored one lasted longer than the gutty.

Writing on March 21st, Horace Hutchinson supported Taylor, and felt that if clubs intended to take away from professionals the right to sell balls, they would have to increase their salaries accordingly. Once again the furore died down quickly and little more was heard on the subject.

The vast majority of professionals made their living looking after golfers and golf courses. Only a few players could earn any substantial money playing in tournaments and exhibitions. Even fewer could make money from designing golf courses. Their main source of income was still from their club jobs, and an important part of that income came from equipment sales: professionals relied on the goodwill of their amateur employers and patrons for their livelihood.

There can be little doubt that the leading professionals earned enough to lead a comfortable life. For instance, Taylor and Vardon were able to afford frequent holidays in Europe. As will be seen, though, the number of leading professionals was relatively few.

An article in the *Glasgow Herald* in February 1911 summed up the structure of professional golf: "Short as the money list is, it is hardly true to say that the prize winners after the leader benefit only to the extent of their money . . . The performances of young players when pitted against the giants of the game are closely watched by club committees in want of a professional, and even a single brilliant performance is often sufficient to bring a valuable appointment. To survive the test of an Open Championship and to finish even among the first dozen is a sufficient recommendation for most committees."

NOTES
1. *Golf Illustrated*, September 1st, 1899
2. *Golf Illustrated*, July 12th, 1907
3. *Golf Illustrated*, December 20th, 1907
4. *Golf*, June 14th, 1895
5. *Golf Illustrated*, February 13th, 1903
6. *Golf Illustrated*, January 10th, 1908
7. *Golf Illustrated*, March 19th, 1909
8. *Golf Illustrated*, June 14th, 1901
9. *Golf Illustrated*, February 4th, 1910
10. *Golf*, December 10th, 1897

3. Exhibition Matches

Harry Vardon in about 1896.

THE LEADING PROFESSIONALS PLAYED A GREAT DEAL of exhibition golf – in the proportion of about three exhibition matches to every tournament. Between 1894 and 1914, Vardon played 544 matches, Taylor 529 and Braid 526. Sandy Herd was involved in 281, George Duncan 187, Ted Ray 177, Ben Sayers 116 and Jack White 109. Whereas the most tournaments that Vardon ever played in a year was 12, he averaged 27 exhibition matches a year, with a high of 53 in 1913. Likewise, Taylor averaged 25 exhibition matches a year (with a peak of 45 in 1910), compared with an average of seven or eight tournaments a year. Braid never played more than 11 tournaments in a year, but also averaged 25 exhibition engagements a year, with a peak of 54 in 1910.

The cycle of exhibition matches was much influenced by who had won the Open Championship. The champion could look forward to a lucrative series of matches both later that same year and the following year. Spectators wanted to see the best players, and a professional had to establish a reputation in tournament play in order to be invited to take part in exhibition matches. Vardon did not play in any matches of note in 1895, and only six in 1896, but his total increased to 16 in 1897 in the wake of his Open win. Herd played in six matches in 1901, and then jumped to 35 in the aftermath of his Open victory in 1902, with a further 24 the following season. Arnaud Massy had played only one match in Britain in 1906, but played 10 in 1907 and a further 20 in 1908. Ted Ray, who won the Open in 1912, took part in only eight matches in 1911, and 32 in 1912 and 56 in 1913 (excluding his tour of America). Jack White could not capitalise on his Open win due to poor health. Winning the *News of the World* Tournament in 1909 helped Tom Ball increase his exhibitions from 7 to 19 in 1910. There was a marked decrease in the total number of exhibition matches in 1900, which can be directly attributed to Vardon, the reigning Champion, spending virtually the whole season in America, and Taylor being there some of the time. The decrease in 1898 can be attributed to the fact that an amateur held the title, and was not available to play exhibition matches.

Earnings from exhibition matches were generally smaller than those from tournaments. Contemporary sources are much less forthcoming about the

Massy wins the Open.

amounts of money that changed hands for exhibition matches than they are about tournaments. H. Ross Coubrough estimated in *Golf Illustrated* that players received an average of £7 per match, less expenses. I had a look at the accounts of 1,667 matches, and could find information about first-place prize in only 46 of them, second prize in 33 and third prize in 17. Excluding challenge matches, on the grounds that the amount of the stake advertised was not – with one exception – going to the players, the total known amount for the 21 years is £1,073.45. Including challenge matches, the total becomes £5,789.55. The average first-place finish of non-challenge matches was worth £14.04, and second place £7.94. Coubrough, in his annual reports in *Golf Illustrated*, intimated that he had access to more figures than he published, and hence how he arrived at a lower figure. As the known figures are such a small percentage of the total, they should be viewed as a rough sample rather than anything like the ultimate truth.

The known figures for Vardon, Taylor, Braid and Herd reinforce the probable value of exhibition play. In six matches, Vardon averaged £16.67 for winning; Taylor £10.46 in seven matches; Braid £15.46 in 17 matches and Herd £14.63 in eight matches. Often an account of a match simply says that the players competed for "a purse of sovereigns". The accounts of challenge matches also confuse the issue. With the probable single exception of Willie Park, the players participating in challenge matches neither put up, nor received, the challenge stakes. They received something for their efforts, but nothing like the full amount of the stake money.

Some definitions

Exhibition matches, as opposed to team matches or tournaments, involved between two and five players. If there were six or more players in an event, I have classified it as a tournament. There are also grey areas as to what constituted a match, as it is sometimes hard to distinguish between an informal meeting of players, one of whom was probably on holiday in the area, and a formal exhibition. However, this would only affect a small percentage of the total.

Tom Ball is seated centre. Also shown are four Open champions: Braid, Massy, Vardon and Herd.

There were three basic formats for exhibition matches. The first was a singles match between two players, which could be either stroke play or match play. Singles was the most common format, and represents just over half the total matches played. These tended to be match play rather than stroke play. However stroke play for singles became quite popular between 1910 and 1914, when almost half the matches played were by strokes. This can simply be attributed to a shift in fashion.

The second format was one where three or four players competed in stroke play. This was a mini tournament, or mini for short.

The third format was foursomes, which account for just over a quarter of the total matches played. They could be either two ball or four ball. Two ball was very popular up to the turn of the century, and then four ball dominated.

Generally speaking, an exhibition event consisted of 36 holes, 18 in the morning and 18 in the afternoon. The match could be a 36-hole singles match or mini event; but more often than not the formats were split. There would be either an 18-hole singles match or mini in the morning, and then possibly a foursomes or a reverse format singles in the afternoon. The foursome was sometimes played first, but, for convenience, the group as a whole are referred to as 'afternoon foursomes'. If a singles match was played first, the two additional players were usually local professionals; if a mini had been played first, the players then just split into two teams.

Afternoon foursomes were played throughout the period, but only started to become popular after 1900, and became a major feature from 1910 onwards. Half of all afternoon foursomes were played between 1910 and 1914. This is part of a fashionable trend and, as will be seen, is also reflected in the growth of foursomes tournaments in the same period.

The playing of reverse format singles in the afternoon in which there was an 18-hole match play match and a separate 18-hole stroke play match became particularly popular from 1908 onwards.

Meanwhile, the amateurs generally could not compete with the leading professionals on the course itself, and they rarely had the opportunity to do so. Amateurs played in 13% of the exhibitions. In singles play, a leading professional played against an amateur a mere 5% of the time, and three-quarters of matches between a professional and an amateur took place between 1894 and 1902. Amateurs played in minis on only five occasions. As is to be expected, amateurs played most frequently in foursomes. Indeed one-third of the total number of foursomes involved at least one amateur.

141 matches were held when a new club or club house was opened, or there was an extended or additional course. At face value this would equate to 11.1% of the new clubs opened in the period. However, as many events were held to celebrate extensions rather than a totally new club, it means that few clubs had the leading professionals play a match in honour of their opening. Opening ceremonies often involved prominent amateurs and occasionally the local professional.

Thus the vast majority of matches were promoted for no special reason except to pit players against each other and entertain the home club members and the public. Whereas taking part in a foursome with a leading professional was undoubtedly a great thrill for the amateur player himself, it was not necessarily popular with the spectators. An irate article in the September 27th, 1907 *Golf Illustrated* complained that spectators did not want to see club members play; they wanted to see the stars.

The professionals gave good value, usually playing their exhibition matches very quickly to fit in the 36 holes. The tee times for the morning and afternoon sessions were often less than four hours apart, and that included a long lunch-break for the spectators and players.

As matches became more and more commonplace throughout the period, especially compared with pre-1893 golf, the line between a challenge match and an exhibition match became increasingly blurred, as it is not clear what the terms of many home and home matches were. However some 43 matches have been classified as challenges, and will be looked at in detail later. Some of these attracted great attention and publicity, but it is important to realise that real challenge matches were but a small part in the development of professional golf in this period.

Gate-money

Although possibly not the first time this had been done, gate-money of 5p was charged for an exhibition match between Vardon and Dalgleish at Nairn on August 15th, 1899, and the practice was castigated in the press. *The Sportsman* claimed: "were the practice of charging a gate to become general, the whole character of the game would be altered", and *The Sporting Life* carried on in the same vein: "No golfer would grudge a shilling to see Vardon perform; it is the principle, not the paying to which he would object." *Golf Illustrated* took a more moderate view and thought that the imposition of gate-money might lead to better crowd control and "would have the desirable effect of increasing the earnings of professional golfers without throwing an additional strain on the exchequers of match promoting clubs".

By 1908, there had been at least six instances when gate-money had been charged, and *Golf Illustrated* expressed great concern over charges for a match between Massy, Taylor and Ben Sayers at the Glasgow North-Western Club. The purpose of the charges was to cover the cost of promoting the match, and any surplus was to be given to charity. The writer saw a day when the matches would start to be run for profit, and ultimately by business syndicates for pure commercial gain. This went against the best interests and traditions of the game. In short, the amateurs would not be able to maintain control of the game.

An admission charge of one shilling (5p) put the game beyond the reach of working class spectators, who were hard-pressed to pay six old pence (2.5p) to watch professional football.

It is hard to gauge the sizes of crowds at these matches. An actual figure was only given in accounts of 55 first-class matches, and even these tended to be estimates. The largest reported crowds were for the £400 Four Greens Foursomes Match in 1905, which attracted 10,000 at St Andrews,

Herd, Taylor, Braid and Vardon before the Great Foursome.

and a total of 26,000 for the four matches. There was a reported crowd of 8,000 at the 1899 Vardon/Park Match. The average of the known crowds was 1,273.

By 1913, there was little doubt that commercial motives had replaced altruistic ones as the main reason for staging exhibition matches. In an editorial in *Golf Illustrated* in 1913, Harold Hilton highlighted the relationship between the promoters and the players: "No attempt indeed is made to disguise the fact that the motives of the promoters is seldom altogether unassociated with some form of advertisement. Nobody knows this better than the leading professionals . . . Naturally the golfer places a somewhat high value upon his services, and as the promoter accedes to the demands made it must naturally be supposed that he cannot be altogether displeased with his bargain." As will be seen, the concept of appearance money is not new and reached a peak during Vardon and Ray's tour of America in 1913.

Between 1910 and 1914 there was a proliferation of exhibition matches, which did not meet with universal approval. A correspondent in the *Daily Mail* in March 1912 wrote: "one possibly does get what might be vulgarly termed 'fed up' by seeing too much really first class golf . . . I must admit to having reached the stage when an exhibition game does not appeal at all." Ernest Lehman in the introduction of the 1913 *Nisbet's Golf Year Book*:

wrote: "In dealing with the professional golf of the year [1912] the reviewer is appalled by the multiplicity and variety of events. Match succeeds match, competition follows competition in an endless procession."

The leading players tended to play exhibition matches in bursts, usually in conjunction with tournament play, and they covered great distances in short periods of time. For example, in 1902, Vardon played Braid on October 3rd at Hythe on the Kent coast, then travelled all night to reach Halifax, Yorkshire, where he defeated Herd the next day, October 4th.

A busy schedule

Vardon's schedule in 1899 was typical for the earlier part of the period. He played a single match in January, which was very unusual, and then began his season in earnest on April 1st, in a tournament at Eastbourne. He played a match a week later in Leicestershire. He then went to Scotland to play in a tournament at Cruden Bay on the 14th, and was back in London by the 20th to play in one at Mid-Surrey. He followed this immediately with an exhibition match, still at Mid-Surrey, and another two days later at Mid-Herts. He played only one match in May – at Porthcawl on the 4th. He played in a match at Raynes Park, London, on June 3rd, and then travelled to Sandwich for the Open, beginning on the 7th. He did not play again until a month later, on July 8th at North Berwick in Scotland. He played four events within seven days in northern England, between the 22nd and 27th of July. He was in Buxton in Derbyshire on August 5th, and then in Scotland playing at Troon, Elie, Leven, Luffness, Nairn, St Andrews and Barnton between August 8th and 19th. Next he crossed over to Ireland to play in a tournament in Portmarnock, beginning on August 31st. A week later he was in Cornwall, playing at Newquay on September 8th. 11 days later he played at Westward Ho! and then on the 30th in Sheffield. On October 7th, he was in Nottingham, and then at West Herts on the 18th and Neasden on the 21st, both in the London area. He finished his year at Brancaster in Norfolk on the 27th.

James Braid's schedule in 1910 is typical of the later period. He played in Northamptonshire on April 7th. Next he played in four events in Scotland between April 16th and April 25th. He played two events in the west of England, on the 3rd and 5th of May, at Burnham and Cirencester, and on the 9th he was in Stockport, before his next appearance in Nottingham on the 26th. He then crossed the Channel to play in the French and Belgian Opens, beginning on June 1st and June 4th respectively. He was back in Britain playing around London on the 9th and 11th, before heading up to Scotland to play in the International Match and the Open. He played in Oban on the 25th, and then Birmingham at the end of the month. Braid was in Woking on July 2nd, before going north yet again to play on Rothesay. Four days later he played in Romford, and two days after that, Colchester; on the 16th he was at Sandy Lodge and on the 20th at Stoke Poges for the *News of the World* Qualifying Tournament. By the end of the month he was in Belgium. There were two events in early August in Scotland, and two late in the month at Deauville. Within ten days in early

September he played in Newcastle, Glasgow and Worsley. There followed a four day period when he was in Brighton and Leeds; he had a week off and then played at Worplesdon. He was inactive for 25 days until October 26th, when he went to Brighton again, and then finished his year in Wales a week later.

In 1914 George Duncan managed to play 43 matches in 27 places, plus seven tournaments, before the end of July. He was touring France in February, and then kicked off his British season on April 2nd. He played only four events and one tournament in England, on the 2nd, 13th, 15th 22nd and 29th. He travelled to Wales to play at Prestatyn on May 2nd, returned to Hertfordshire to play in a tournament on the 6th, and then went to Monifieth in Scotland to play an event on the 9th. He was back in the London area, playing in a tournament, on the 13th, and then an exhibition event on the 16th. He went to Wales again on the 20th and 21st. On the 23rd he played in Lancaster, on the 25th in a tournament at Port Seton in Scotland, and on the 28th he was in Cheshire. He was at Kingsknowe in Scotland on the 30th, and Cruden Bay on June 2nd. He had a rest until the Open at Prestwick, starting on June 18th, and then he played in four events in Scotland within a week after the Open finished. There followed an exhibition match at Maidstone in Kent on his way to Le Touquet, for the French Open. He caught his breath, and next played on July 20th at Seaham Harbour, followed by Prestwich, Hornsea and Falkirk in Scotland between then and the 27th.

The leading players had a gruelling schedule that became progressively harder as the number of exhibition events and tournaments steadily increased in the years just before the war. It obviously put a great strain on the players. The editor of *Golf* commended Vardon for sustaining a long spell of excellent golf in 1898, and he wrote on September 16th "most first class players get stale in a few weeks after getting to the top of their games, especially under the strain of a succession of big matches." Vardon himself felt the pressure, and was quoted in 1903 as saying "I find the game a great strain. We never get a rest, and when you've got to keep up your reputation, every match has a wearing effect, for from the beginning to the end you have no relief of the tension."[1] In 1908 a writer noted "The professional golfer of today requires in addition to superlative skill, a constitution of iron to stand the strain."[2]

Were they trying?

With the number of engagements that they undertook, there were rumours that the professionals were not always trying. These surfaced as early as January 1897 in *Golf*. Taylor was allowed to write a rebuttal on January 15th in which he categorically denied that he had been involved in a match in which any player gave less than 100% effort, and he regarded his reputation as a golfer to be more important than pleasing a crowd, and more valuable than any stake money for which he had played. The thought lingered on, and Vardon felt that he had to mention it in his book *The Complete Golfer* in 1905. He wrote: "We dare not play tricks with such rep-

George Duncan's free-flowing swing.

utations as we may have had the good fortune to obtain." They always did their utmost to play their best. In 1908 there was another rumour that the Triumvirate had agreed to pool their prize money in the *News of the World* Tournament. This was heavily quashed in *Golf Illustrated* on October 16th.

The training methods of the leading players were rather crude. J.H. Taylor prepared for the 1910 season by working out with a punch-ball and boxing. Braid was a believer in regular work habits, a regular amount of exercise and a lot of sleep. He did not smoke and drank very little. In 1905 Vardon wrote that he did not believe in training. However, as the effects of tuberculosis wore on, he found that he did. His preparation for the 1911 Open was described in detail by C.B. Macfarlane in the July 7th *Golf Illustrated*. Vardon had been preparing for the Open for five months by following a regime set by a Dr Belding. He was put on a strict diet, and only allowed one whisky and four pipes a day. He worked out by playing two rounds of golf a day, plus walking 12 miles, and he was not allowed to use a punching-bag or weights.

Herd prepared for the 1902 Open by concentrating on the mental aspects of the game. He was taken in hand by two amateur players, D.S. Crowther and Sir Charles Sykes. They played a variety of courses in northern England, with Herd giving his "trainers" liberal handicaps to force him to concentrate better. He reached the stage where he was "playing like a machine", so he reduced his programme so that he would not peak too soon. Three weeks before the Open he resumed serious practice, to reach "the pitch of perfection", making no changes in his regular habits except "greater regularity in food and sleep".

Vardon and Taylor in c. 1905.

Golfing wear

Vardon was responsible for setting the trend of wearing knickerbockers and stockings instead of ordinary trousers, in about 1898. In 1905, *Golf Illustrated* noted the great improvement in the appearance of professional golfers in contrast to the "old days when a professional could always be distinguished by his slouching gait, and too often, by the out-at-elbows state of his garments". In the same issue it was reported that the veteran Andrew Kirkaldy was amazed when he went to a hotel reception and said, "I saw a sight I never thought t'see in my life – a professional in a tail coat!"³

In 1911, *Golf Illustrated* listed the leading professionals who wore ordinary trousers and those who wore knickerbockers. The traditionalists were Taylor, Braid, Herd, Ray, Willie Park, Andrew Kirkaldy, Ben Sayers, Arnaud Massy, James Sherlock and Fred Robson. The trend-setters were Harry and Tom Vardon, George Duncan, Charles Mayo, Tom Ball and P.J. Gaudin.⁴

Finally, Vardon, ever the stylist, recommended that any golfer should "always use braces in preference to a belt round the waist. I never play with a belt. Braces seem to hold the shoulders together just as they ought to be. When a man plays in a belt he has an unaccustomed sense of looseness and his shoulders are too much beyond control . . . I do not advise a golfer to play without his coat, even on the warmest day, if he wants to play his best game." Obviously this is where modern players have been going wrong!

Harry Vardon in knicker-bockers.

Vardon and Braid, in c. 1905.

Team matches

One of the more interesting developments, which shows how the game was spreading, and was another form of competitive exhibition match, was that of team matches. These divide into two basic categories, regional/local professional matches and professional *versus* amateur matches. Little or no money was at stake in these matches.

The Midlands Counties began holding a regular pro/am match in 1905, when the professionals won by a score of 11 to 8. Players of the calibre of Williamson, Sherlock, Cawsey and Coburn played for the professionals.

J.H. Taylor drives, watched by James Braid (leaning on his club) in c. 1903.

The Irish Professionals played the Irish Amateurs starting in 1908, and the Yorkshire Professionals are reported as playing the Yorkshire Amateurs the following year.

There were two matches, one in 1909 and one in 1910, when the gentlemen of the press took on the might of the professionals. The matches were played under handicap, with the professionals all rated at plus 6, while the amateurs played to their best club handicap. The professionals won easily on both occasions. A strong professional team also turned out to play the Oxford and Cambridge Golfing Society at Stoke Poges in January 1911. Play was foursomes, and all the amateurs received a start of two holes. Using this advantage, they won the match. In 1913 the society played another professional team, which included Taylor, Braid, Duncan, Herd, Ball, Sherlock and Mayo, at the opening of St George's-on-the-Hill, and lost.

Regional, and then local, rivalries brought about further professional matches. Yorkshire and Lancashire teams began playing one another in 1906. By 1914 Kent, Sussex, Durham, Northumberland, Gloucestershire and Somerset professionals had all held team competitions. Ted Ray and Sandy Herd both played regularly for Yorkshire, until they moved south, while Tom Renouf was a stalwart regular for Lancashire.

Finally there comes the question to which everyone wants to know the answer concerning exhibition matches. How did the Triumvirate do against each other in head-to-head singles combat in exhibition matches? The answer is as follows:

Vardon *versus* Taylor

Vardon and Taylor played each other 47 times. Vardon won 26, Taylor won 19 and they halved twice.

Vardon *versus* Braid

Vardon and Braid played each other 83 times. Vardon won 36, Braid won 40 times and they halved seven.

Braid *versus* Taylor

Braid and Taylor played each other 74 times. They each won 31 and halved 12.

Therefore Vardon had an edge over Taylor, as did Braid over Vardon, while Taylor and Braid were dead level.

NOTES
1. *Golf Illustrated,* August 7th, 1903
2. *Golf Illustrated,* March 27th, 1908
3. *Golf Illustrated,* June 16th, 1905
4. *Golf Illustrated,* October 13th, 1911

4. High-stake Matches, 1894-1914

Edward Hulton.

AS HAS BEEN SHOWN, EXHIBITION MATCHES WERE the bread and butter of the leading professionals' competitive lives. They were played frequently, if a player had acquired a sufficient reputation in tournament play. They provided a steady, if not spectacular, supplement to professionals' income. Most exhibition matches were played for relatively little in the way of prize money and received little publicity. The press reports of the weekly doings of the professionals usually ran to one or two paragraphs. The matches that excited the contemporary journalists were those played for high stakes, and generally fell under the heading of 'challenge matches'.

Challenge matches are generally misunderstood. They were played for big stakes, usually provided by wealthy backers and not by the players themselves. The players stood to win some money, but rarely the sum of the stake. The size of the stake is also often misconstrued.

Of the leading professionals, it is probable that only Willie Park put up his own money. In his £100 match against Park in 1894, Douglas Rolland was backed by George Newnes, who put up the stake money. The agreement was that Rolland would receive £15 if he won and nothing if he lost. Newnes backed Taylor against Park in 1896, and the account in *Golf* stated that Park put up his own money.

In the 1905 £400 Foursome Match in which Vardon and Taylor opposed Braid and Herd, the English pair were staked by Edward Hulton and the Scottish pair by George Riddell. The terms of this match are quite interesting, for both Hulton and Riddell actually put up £200 each, so each stood to win the other's £200. It was journalistic licence to say that it was a £400 match; the total stakes came to that, but the loser would pay out £200 and the winner would receive that plus the £200 which already belonged to him. This was the normal state of affairs in challenge matches. The same article, on August 4th, 1905, states that, although there is no mention of this in the formal agreement, "there is a private arrangement, by grace of the backers, that the winning players are to benefit very considerably from the stake money. The losers will receive nothing." A correspondent in *The Manchester Guardian* feigned a great lack of interest in these stake money matches, and he wrote in February 1901, with regard to a White/Taylor match, "it seems odd that one should be expected to make a special fuss over it because the men have a bet of £50 on the result."

In a 1906 match of Duncan and Mayo against Vardon and Braid, the former pair's stake money of £50 was put up by "a third party". Duncan and Mayo's arrangement was that if they won they would receive £50, and if they lost they would not receive anything.

It was reported in 1908 that "there has lately been some criticism of these professional stake matches on the lines that they are gladiatorial shows which do no good to the game."[1] The writer disagreed with this criticism because ordinary exhibition matches, where the leading professional played for a fixed fee, lacked the atmosphere of challenge matches. However he wanted the players to put up their own money, otherwise "the match would be degraded below the level of an ordinary exhibition match and would excite only the faintest interest." Yet what evidence there is suggests that the players rarely played for their own money. The big money matches excited the public and the press far more than the normal exhibition matches, and there were far fewer of them.

Big money matches, 1894–1897

There were two big money matches with stakes of £50 or more in 1894. The first was the aforementioned £50-a-side match between Rolland and Park at Sandwich, which Rolland won by 3 and 2. The second was the £50-a-side match between Andrew Kirkaldy and Ben Sayers, which Sayers won by 2 holes. Kirkaldy issued the challenge, and stipulated that the match had to be played at Prestwick, St Andrews or Carnoustie. Taylor was interested in playing him, but wanted one of the courses to be in England. As Kirkaldy's "supporters" would not change the conditions, the negotiations fell through. The terms were altered for Sayers, and the match was played at St Andrews and North Berwick.

Three big money matches took place in 1895, and one was abandoned. In April Herd played Alfred Toogood at Minchinhampton and Huddersfield for £100 a side. A witness criticised the Huddersfield members (who were staking the match) for sending Herd to Minchinhampton on his own, "with not a soul to encourage him or to keep his spirits up as the play went on".[2]

The second match was for £50 a side, and was between Taylor and Kirkaldy. This time it was Taylor who issued the challenge, taking out an advertisement in the May 17th *Golf*. This stated that he was willing to play any professional at St Andrews during the championship week. The acceptance was to be made through the editor of *Golf*, and the money had to be lodged with him by June 8th. The 36-hole match was square with four to play. At the 15th hole, Taylor outdrove Kirkaldy by 25 yards, but was off line and had a poor lie. Kirkaldy used a wood for his second shot, reached the green and was down in four, while Taylor needed five. Taylor was still one down at the 18th, and was short with his approach shot. His 30-yard putt failed by less than an inch, and Kirkaldy, halving the hole, emerged the winner.

Shortly after the Open, Kirkaldy and Archie Simpson issued a challenge to play any two professionals over three Scottish greens. Taylor and Herd wanted to accept the challenge, but to play it later in the year. The Scottish pair, however, wanted to play it immediately, as several officers at the army camp in Barry wanted to stake Taylor and Herd, but only if the match could be played before their camp broke in a fortnight's time. Taylor did not feel that he could travel back to Scotland, having only just returned home, so the match did not take place. However Taylor and Herd issued a challenge the next year to the Scottish pair, but again the match did not take place. The third challenge match of 1895 was played in October, with Kirkaldy taking on Willie Fernie over Troon, Prestwick and St Andrews. Fernie emerged the winner.

There were two major money matches in 1896. The first was the £50-a-side match between Taylor and Park at Musselburgh and Sudbrook Park, Richmond. In the first leg, at Musselburgh, Taylor had problems throughout with putting. Although Park was plagued by hooked drives, his short game was firing on all cylinders, and he took a four hole lead for the day. They met nine days later on June 27th, and both men were now on form. Taylor knocked two holes off Park's lead in the first round. They reached the penultimate hole with Park clinging to a lead of one hole. Taylor looked as if he would tie the match, after Park badly sliced his brassie shot towards a cluster of trees, while the Englishman hit his second straight to the green. As luck would have it, Park's shot hit a tree and rebounded into the middle of the course, leaving him a clear line to the green. He was able to halve the hole. At the short 18th hole, Taylor made a gallant effort to hole his second shot using his mashie, but at the last moment the ball made a right turn and missed the hole by three inches. Park was once again able to get the half, and thereby won the match.

Taylor's backer for this match, George Newnes, was an active patron of the game. He is mentioned as having put up a prize of £20 at three ordinary exhibition matches: Herd versus Taylor and Herd versus White, both in 1896; and Vardon and Taylor versus Braid and Herd in 1899.

The second big match of 1896 was between Sayers and Herd. The former issued the challenge, and it was hoped that an English player would accept; but only the fellow Scot, Sandy Herd, took him up. The Huddersfield-based professional won handily, by a score of 13 and 12.

The only major challenge in 1897 was a match between Kirkaldy and A.H. Scott, played at Earlsferry and St Andrews for £50 a side. The match was most notable for the poor behaviour of the St Andrews crowd. As the close-fought match neared the end "the crowd, numbering some thousands of persons, behaved extremely badly; being apparently lost to all sense of decency and fair play."[3] Even Kirkaldy was bothered by their lack of restraint, and their surging in masses all over the line of play, but he held on to his lead and won 3 and 1.

The high point
In many respects challenge matches reached a high point in 1898 and 1899. There were three big money matches in 1898, and the beginning of the

Park against Fernie at Musselburgh in 1898.

negotiations for a match that took nearly a year to come to fruition. In April 1898 Sayers and Simpson took on Kirkaldy and Herd at Aberdeen and St Andrews for £50 a side. The latter pair won handily 12 and 11. Apparently Simpson did not wish to play out the bye, and Kirkaldy sympathised with him, saying "It's nae use hammerin' your guts out and get nothin' for it." The next month Park defeated Fernie by 13 and 12 in a £50-a-side match over Musselburgh and Troon. The match was notable for the pair being filmed at the first tee by a local "cinematographer".

In October, Taylor defeated Kirkaldy at Brancaster in Norfolk in an exhibition match and won £50. Apparently the money had been raised as Kirkaldy's stake money for a challenge match against Vardon which the Open champion did not to accept due to other commitments.

In the wake of his one-stroke defeat in the 1898 Open, Willie Park challenged Vardon to a £100-a-side match over Musselburgh and any other seaside course the next month, August. Park's challenge was based more on emotion than sound judgement. Park had been playing relatively little competitive golf. Since the start of 1894, the best he had done in tournaments was to finish second twice, at Aberdeen in 1896 and at the 1898 Open. Over the same period Vardon had won 19 tournaments. Park had played five exhibition matches in 1897, winning four, while Vardon played 14, winning 10. In 1898, Park played three, winning all of them, while Vardon played six, winning three. In 1899, Park played three matches prior to the two with Vardon, while Vardon played four. Significantly, Park had not played an exhibition match outside Scotland since 1896, and of his 11 matches in 1897, 1898 and 1899, seven of them were against Ben Sayers, two against Willie Fernie, and one against John Laidlay and Robert Maxwell, both of whom were amateurs. In the same three-year period, Vardon played 24 matches, all over Britain, and faced Braid six times, Herd five times and Taylor three times. In short, Vardon was playing more golf against tougher opposition than Park.

Nevertheless, such was Park's reputation that Vardon replied a week later that he would play for £50 a side, and the match had to be over two neutral courses, namely St Andrews and Sandwich. Negotiations broke down, and on August 26th, Park issued a new challenge to "play anyone a four-green [match], 36 holes over each, for £100 a side each man to select two greens and the match to be played in October". There was little doubt in the golfing world that the target for this new challenge was Harry Vardon. Apparently Vardon did not want to play Park over Musselburgh. At the same time Kirkaldy challenged Vardon to play at Brancaster on October 11th. Vardon said he could play on the 26th but not the 11th – hence the availability of the £50 prize for which Kirkaldy and Taylor played.

Park found no takers for his four-greens challenge, and he wrote to *Golf* on November 15th that he was "prepared to play Harry Vardon over North Berwick and any other green (36 holes each) for £100 a side. The match is to take place in the spring of the year and each man to deposit £25 for the purpose of binding the match." Vardon wrote back on November 21st that he accepted the challenge, and chose Ganton as the other course. Park suggested the first week in July at North Berwick, and two weeks later at Ganton; Vardon accepted in the December 2nd *Golf*.

Willie Park putting, at the final green in the 1898 Open.

Opposite: Jack White, 1904.

The match finally took place in 1899 on July 8th and 22nd. The crowd at North Berwick, which swelled to 8,000, included the Prince of Wales. Shops were shut for the afternoon round, and a special telegraph hotline was set up by which the latest score could be obtained for 7.5p.

At North Berwick, in a remarkable sequence, the first 10 holes were halved, and at the end of the first round Park led by a single hole. Vardon squared the match at the 1st hole of the second round, when Park pulled his drive and was unable to sink his long putt. Park regained the lead at the next hole, when Vardon missed a five-foot putt; but Vardon drew level at the 3rd hole. They stayed level until the 9th hole, when Park once again hooked his drive. Vardon further increased his lead at the 10th, when Park put his approach shot into a bunker. The Scotsman came straight back to take the next two holes, helped by some weak putting by Vardon. At the 13th, Park put his iron tee shot next to the wall and took an extra shot to clear it, giving Vardon the hole. Park then tied the match yet again at the 14th, when Vardon putted poorly. At the 15th Park failed to clear the bunker guarding the hole and Vardon took the lead, which he extended at the 16th, when Park took two strokes to clear the dry ditch. The day ended with two halves and Vardon up by two holes.

At Ganton the tone of the day was set when, at the 1st hole, Vardon drove straight down the middle, while Park hooked his tee shot into a bunker. Vardon was quickly up by three. He won the 3rd hole to go four up, but Park pulled one back at the 4th. Poor driving cost Park the 5th and 6th holes, and a missed putt the 7th. He was now six down. He went seven down at the 11th, when he was short with his tee shot, while Vardon was down in two, having placed his shot within 12 feet of the pin. Park won the 14th hole, but lost the next two, to finish the first round down by eight. The last round was academic. Park continued to play poorly and Vardon wonderfully. Park crashed to defeat by a margin of 11 and 10.

End of an era

In many ways the match marked the end of an era, as challenge matches now declined in popularity. The main participants in many of the challenges played up to 1899 – Kirkaldy, Sayers and Park – were rapidly passing their peaks as players. Jack White, who was Sayers' nephew by marriage, kept the tradition going, but without a great deal of personal success. Challenges only really revived with the coming of a new generation of players around 1906.

In 1901 Jack White challenged J.H. Taylor to a £50-a-side match, which was duly played on May 4th at Mid-Surrey and May 25th at Huntercombe. Taylor won 4 and 3. The next year Tom Vardon challenged White to a £50-a-side match, played at Sandwich on October 18th and Sunningdale on November 1st. White lost again, this time by a score of 2 and 1, with both players using the rubber-cored ball. The dearth of challenge matches was remarked upon in the accounts of both legs. Indeed, challenge matches were referred to as "a rare thing nowadays", and a refreshing change from "these days of exhibition golf".[4]

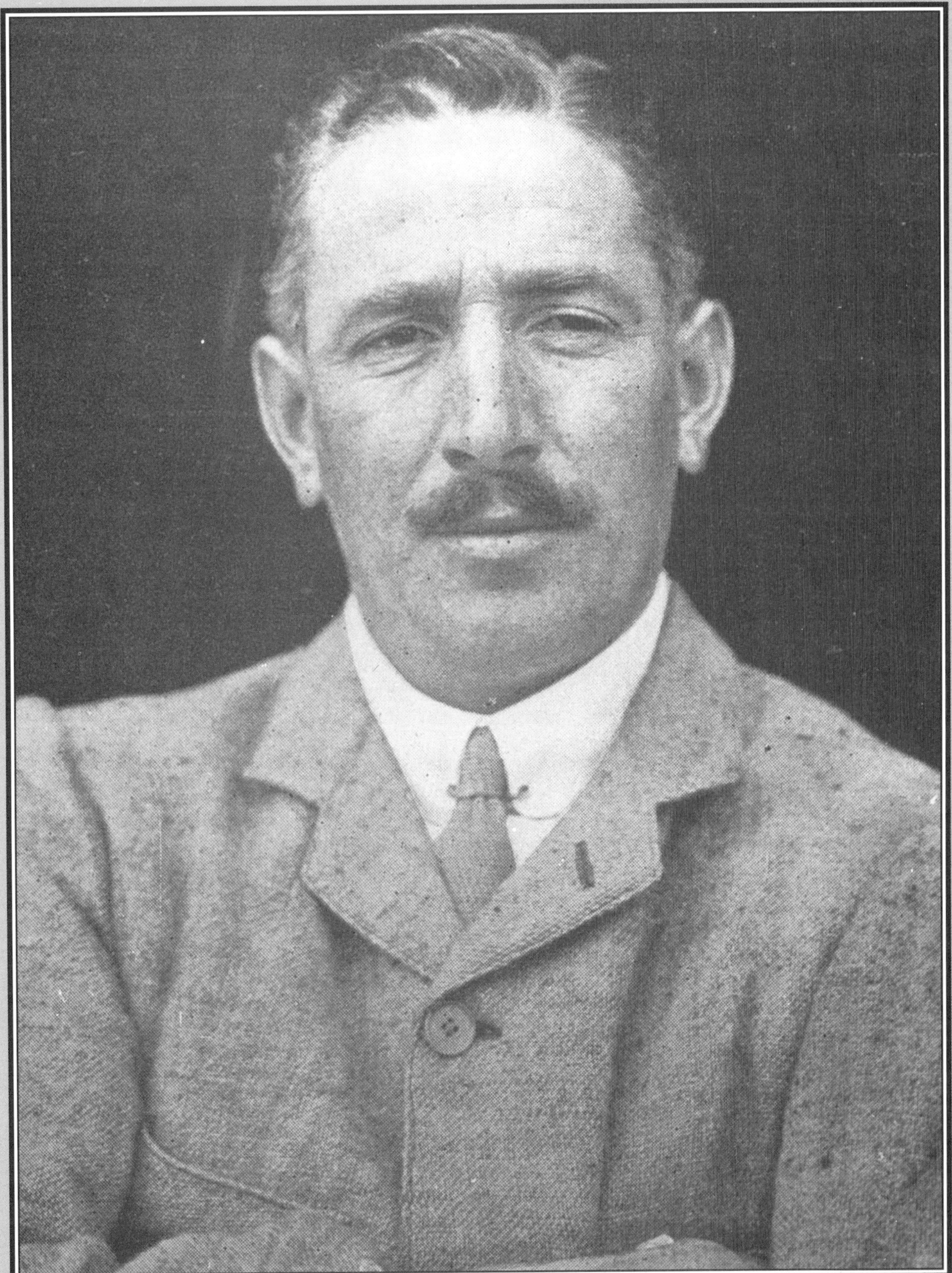

They stayed rare; the next big-money match was not until 1905 – and it was not a challenge match. In June 1905, Frank Kinloch suggested that an international foursome (i.e. England and Scotland) should be played over four greens for substantial money stakes.[5] This suggestion immediately found favour, and Edward Hulton, hiding under the pseudonym of "W.L.S.", offered to put up a stake of £200 for the English pair, and George Riddell, keeping equally anonymous, backed the Scottish pair. The English team was Vardon and Taylor. At first the Scottish team was to be Braid and Park, but the latter had too many business commitments and Herd was chosen to replace him. Hulton had specified that one of the courses had to be St Anne's, and the other three courses chosen were Deal, St Andrews and Sunningdale. Sunningdale was quickly replaced by Troon, so that there would be two English and two Scottish courses. The first 36 holes were to be played at St Andrews on August 23rd, the next 36 at Troon on August 30th, then came St Anne's on September 5th, with the final 36 at Deal on September 9th. The scores were to be kept cumulatively over the 144 holes.

International foursomes

The original choice of Willie Park to play with Braid was more emotional than sensible. Park, twice Open champion in the 1880s, had only played in seven foursome matches since 1894, and three of those were the PGA International Matches in 1903, 1904 and 1905. Altogether he had won four and lost three. His replacement, Sandy Herd, had played in 44 in the same period, 1894 to August 20th, 1905. His team-mate, Braid, had played in 76 foursomes, while Vardon had played in 56 matches, and Taylor 77.

On paper, the team of Herd and Braid appeared to be the favourites. They had played the English pair 14 times between 1898 and August 1905, and had won six of the contests. Vardon and Taylor had won three times, but two of those victories had been back in 1899. The remaining five matches were halved. They had already met twice in 1905, playing against one another in the International Match in St Andrews on June 3rd, halving their match; and then again the same month in Newquay, Cornwall, where the two Scotsmen won by 3 and 1.

Braid was in the midst of a purple run in tournament play. He had played in six tournaments up to August 1905, winning three, including the Open, and finishing no lower than fourth. Herd had played in four, winning two that year. Taylor had played in six, finishing second in four, third in one and reaching the semifinal in the other. Vardon had played in seven tournaments, winning one, coming second in one, and finishing third or fourth in four. His putting had become very suspect since his illness in 1903. The final advantage for the Scots was that the first two rounds were to be played in Scotland.

The match attracted great interest in advance, being heavily promoted, and receiving unprecedented coverage in Golf Illustrated, far in excess of that given to even the Open and Amateur Championships. There were hole-by-hole descriptions and diagrams showing how the holes were won and lost.

1st Leg – St Andrews, August 23rd

Fittingly, the match began in St Andrews, on August 23rd, with a crowd of 10,000 watching. Tom Morris, "the surviving hero of the last £400 foursome" was introduced to the crowd and given a seat near the starter's box. Forty stewards and "a small battalion" of police were needed to control the crowds. A blue flag was raised when England won a hole, a yellow one when Scotland won, and both flags when a hole was halved.

Scotland drew first blood when Vardon left Taylor a 12-foot putt at the 2nd hole which Taylor was unable to sink. The English pair squared the match at the 5th, when Herd pulled his drive and Braid was short with his approach shot. The Scottish team went back into the lead at the 8th, when Vardon missed a six-foot putt. They went two up at the 9th, when Taylor was short with a nine-foot putt and Braid worked his way around a half stymie to take the hole. The Englishmen cut the lead to one hole at the 13th, despite Taylor topping his drive and Vardon pulling his approach shot. However the Scotsmen came back and were three up at the end of the first round, mainly through excellent approach work to the greens. Vardon and Taylor came back and squared the match at the 26th hole, the holes being won and lost on the greens.

This turned out to be the end of the English challenge for the day. At the 27th, Vardon missed a two-foot putt to give the Scots the lead again, which they held for the rest of the match, finishing two up on the day. Herd and Braid were hoisted onto several hefty pairs of Scottish shoulders and carried off the course in triumph. Vardon had found the highly partisan crowd at St Andrews very distracting, and, according to Taylor, more than once threatened to walk off the course.

2nd Leg – Troon, August 30th

Herd and Braid's advantage rapidly disappeared at Troon. The start of the match gave no indication of what was to come. It looked as if the see-saw battle of the previous week would continue. The Scots won the first hole of the day, which was the 37th of the match. But things began to go wrong for the Scottish pair at the 42nd hole. The English team won it, courtesy of Taylor's magnificent brassie shot to the green, to cut the deficit to two holes. Braid put his tee shot in the bunker at the next hole, and Herd was unable to get out in one; now their lead was down to one hole. The Englishmen tied the match at the 44th hole, when Braid's approach shot was short and stuck in the bank guarding the green. They won the next hole, to take the lead for the first time; but the Scots came back at the 46th to tie the match. Poor play by both Herd and Braid cost them the next hole, and they went one down. Vardon's 24-foot putt earned the pair the next hole, to go two up, and by the 50th hole they were four up – a lead they held at the end of the round.

The second round was a rout that turned into a massacre. A magnificent second shot by Vardon at the 55th hole left the ball within five feet of the pin, and the English pair went five up. Taylor returned the favour at the 56th, and left Vardon with a four-foot putt, making them six up. Herd missed a short putt at the next and the Scots were now seven down. The Scottish pair won the next hole, but the English lead was back to seven after the 59th hole. At the 61st hole the two Englishmen went eight up, when Braid played a poor approach shot, Herd putted poorly and Braid's putt was even worse. The English team went nine up at the 64th hole, courtesy of another bad approach shot by Herd, and 10 up at the 65th when Braid missed a three-foot putt. The English pair went 11 up at the 68th hole and 12 up at the 72nd, the Scots losing both holes through being short both off the tee and with their approach shots. Needless to say, the crowd of 5,000 were not best pleased by the events of the day, which effectively put an end to the overall contest.

The result that day stunned the Scottish golfing public. Vardon felt that he and Taylor played the best golf of their careers. He attributed his success to his cleek shots, calling it the outstanding feature of his play. According to Taylor, a story soon circulated that Herd and Braid had been drugged the night before, when all four players had dined with Fred Billington, a star of the D'Oyly Carte Opera Company (the leading performers of Gilbert and Sullivan). He dismissed this out of hand. Herd produced a somewhat more plausible excuse. He had an infected knee, and Braid was suffering from the flu. The day's play was best summed up by a story told by Vardon. There was an eclipse of the sun during the match. An old lady spectator was asked if she had seen it, and replied "I don't know about the eclipse of the sun, but I have this day seen the eclipse of Scotland."

3rd Leg – St Anne's September 5th

The four resumed battle six days later at St Anne's. Things got worse for the Scottish pair before they got better. By the 78th hole they were 15 down, but they began to recover at the 82nd hole, when Herd holed a 45-foot putt to reduce the deficit to 13. Then the Huddersfield professional sank a 36-foot putt at the 84th hole to trail by 12. The Scots took the 87th hole, after Taylor sliced his drive. The English duo took the 91st hole, to restore the 12-hole advantage. Herd holed another long putt to take the 97th hole, and again at the 99th hole, to reduce the lead to 10. The Scots took the 100th hole, after Vardon hooked his drive, and the 101st when Taylor missed a six-foot putt. Taylor's errant second shot cost the English the 104th hole, and their lead was now seven holes. That was the difference at the end of the day. The Scots had taken five holes off the overall lead.

After the first round, the four players had gone back to their hotel for lunch, and were refused admission back on to the course by a policeman because they did not have badges which signified that they had paid their admission charge. The policeman would not relent, even when they explained who they were and that, if he didn't let them in, there would not be any play. They were finally allowed to pass when others vouched for them and told the policeman that they were indeed the four contestants.

Sandy Herd dressed up for the photographer, *c.* **1892.**

Last Leg – Deal, September 9th

Any hopes of a miraculous Scottish comeback were dashed in the wind and rain at Deal. However, Vardon almost did not make it to the course. The night before he suffered another recurrence of his illness and had been haemorrhaging. Fortunately, he recovered by the morning.

On the first hole of the day, and the 109th overall, Braid put his tee shot into the rough and Herd could not reach the green. The English lead was back to eight and was increased to nine at the 110th, when Herd sliced his tee shot into the rough and Braid missed a three-foot putt for the half. The English pair then went 10 up at the 115th, when, after Vardon had put the approach shot past the fence on the far side of the green, Taylor was able to pitch it stone dead. Braid hit his approach shot too strongly at the 120th hole, and the English lead went up to 11. It increased to 12 at the next hole, when Taylor sank a 36-footer for a three. At the end of the first round they were 13 up, and they were still 13 up, and the victors, with 12 holes to play.

Despite the final score, the match was deemed a great success. It was estimated that 26,000 spectators witnessed the four matches and that the players travelled 1,200 miles in the process. John Low had acted as the match referee, and, when it was all over, each of the four players gave Low as a wedding present one of the clubs they had used.[6] We do not have a record of the future Mrs Low's reaction to this gift.

Vardon later referred to the match as one of the biggest events of his golfing life. Vardon, Taylor and Herd all gave detailed accounts of it in their autobiographies, which reflected how important each one of them felt the event had been. The day's play in Troon continued to bother Herd. He wrote in 1923 "if anybody wanted to raise my dander afterwards they had only to ask 'What sort o' course is Troon, Sandy, that ye made sich a hash o' it there?'" The popularity of the match was an undoubted spur to the popularity of foursomes tournaments from 1906 onwards.

More challenge matches

The next big money challenge match did not take place until November 1906. George Duncan and Charles Mayo issued a challenge, accepted by Vardon and Braid, to play a £50-a-side foursomes match at Walton Heath and Timperley. The challenge was criticised because it had not come from the players themselves: "One cannot help regretting . . . the lack of initiative among the professionals themselves, and the absence of the keen personal rivalry which used to inspire the old matches and make them worth following."[7] Further controversy followed quickly when it was announced that the Timperley Club was to charge 12.5p admission for non-members. The promoters of the match were "furious with the Timperley Club for taking a step which threatens to deter the public from attending the final, and thus to a large extent defeat the objects they have in view".[8] Braid and Vardon went 4 up at Walton Heath, and increased that lead at Timperley, where some 1,500 spectators turned up, to win by 9 and 8. This victory helped produce a profit of £40, which was handed over to charity.[9]

In 1907 there was a Braid *versus* Massy match which was not quite a challenge match. After Massy won the Open and the French Open in 1907, it was felt that it was inevitable "that sooner or later some one of our leading pro's, smarting under their successive defeats at the hands of Massy, should challenge him to single combat". The writer went on to remind readers that "the Open Champion is never allowed to rest on his laurels, and though he is chiefly engaged in exhibition games, the winning or losing of which do not add, or detract much from, his reputation, he is always open to a challenge of a more serious nature for a money stake."[10]

Such a challenge came from Braid "who has been backed to play the Open Champion for £100". Braid wanted to play over St Andrews and Deal. Massy held out for the Scottish green to be North Berwick, and in

The big foursome for £200: George Duncan, J.H. Taylor, James Braid and C.H. Mayo.

England preferred Hoylake to Deal. Deadlock ensued, and the August 9th *Golf Illustrated* suggested that they play over Walton Heath and North Berwick, which were the players' home courses. The following week it was reported that no further progress had been made in resolving the issue of venues, and "it can only be hoped that some compromise, or alternative, may be arrived at, and that the year will not be allowed to close without so sporting and interesting a fixture being arranged."

Meanwhile, Ted Ray also challenged Massy to a £100-a-side match over Ganton and North Berwick. The Frenchman declined, saying that he wished to play Braid first. Massy returned to France on September 20th, having said that he did not think he would play Braid until at least April 1908. However, it was then announced in the November 22nd, 1907 *Golf Illustrated* that Massy and Braid were to play a match at Deal on December

19th. This match was not the challenge match, but one for "a substantial purse, privately subscribed". Nevertheless it was viewed by the public and the press as if it were a challenge match.

Braid took the 1st hole, when Massy pulled his drive, and then the 3rd hole, when he hit a blind approach shot stone dead and held his lead going into the turn. Braid's good work for the morning was partially undone at the 17th and 18th holes, where poor approaching and worse putting resulted in a pair of sixes and the loss of two holes of his lead, leaving him only one up.

Braid had out-driven Massy all morning, but now, possibly refreshed by his lunch, the Frenchman began to assert his power off the tee. He squared the match when his mashie shot pitched into the hole for a three at the 1st hole. Another beautiful pitch at the 3rd gave Massy the lead for the first time. Braid squared it again at the 4th, only to throw it away at the 5th, with more poor putting. Massy then won the 8th hole, to go two up at the turn. The match was settled at the 15th hole, when Massy hit a daring high-cut approach shot on to the green, which gave him the hole. Although Braid reduced the deficit at the 16th hole back to two, a half at the 17th ended the match in Massy's favour by 2 and 1.

A triple crown?
The Liverpool Daily Courier reported that "the Frenchman has gained the triple crown of victory". *The Daily Chronicle* told its readers that "although the Scotsman was at one time four holes up, Massy played better and secured a victory that will live long as one of the most memorable in the history of the game." *The Globe* reporter felt that "if the match had been for £1,000, it could not have produced a more interesting contest."

Massy did not play Braid again in April 1908. Instead there was a match, but not a challenge one, with Harry Vardon, again at Deal. Vardon won easily by 9 and 7. All the superlatives written about the Frenchman five months earlier were quickly forgotten, proving that the short memory of the sports journalist is no new phenomenon.

There was one large-purse challenge match in 1908, a foursome played over Deal and Prince's, Sandwich, in November. George Duncan and Charles Mayo defeated Ted Ray and Tom Vardon by 6 and 5. Duncan and Mayo must have been an interesting pair to watch: Duncan had the reputation of playing golf at the gallop, while Mayo had the reputation of playing at a crawl, and was viewed as the most deliberate and slowest of the leading players. Presumably they combined to play at a medium pace!

Duncan and Mayo immediately issued an open challenge to play any two golfers for £100-a-side. This was accepted by Braid and Taylor, and played at Burhill and Walton Heath on April 24th and April 29th, 1909. The pair of champions took a five-hole lead at Burhill (Mayo's home course), and went on to secure victory at Walton Heath by 8 and 7. After the match, Garden Smith wrote that "the effect of this match will probably be that Braid and Taylor, or any two of the Triumvirate, are left severely alone by the younger generation for some time to come."[11] That is precisely what

James Sherlock in 1910.

happened. None of the Triumvirate played another major challenge match before the outbreak of war in 1914. The challenges were left for the younger players.

In June 1909, Mayo played Peter Rainford for £50-a-side at Burhill and Llangammarch Wells, and Mayo won by 13 and 12. J.D. Edgar, who was to cause a sensation by winning the 1913 French Open, halved a £25-a-side match with J.W. Gaudin in September of the same year.

A golden age?
In 1911 Jack White challenged James Sherlock, the 1910 *News of the World* Champion, to a £50-a-side match, and, as normal, poor Jack lost. This time it was by a margin of 14 and 12, at Stoke Poges and Sunningdale.

The absence of first class-challenge matches bred a nostalgia for a lost "golden age". This, in turn, led to the first "old-timers'", or seniors', match when, in November 1911, Andrew Kirkaldy and Ben Sayers were staked to a £50-a-side 72-hole match, to be played over Sunningdale and Walton Heath. By now Kirkaldy was 51 and Sayers 54. The match account in *Golf Illustrated* on November 17th, written by Ernest Lehman, is disproportionately long in comparison to the actual significance of the match. He continually harked back to bygone days, and felt the match "showed us two splendid veterans who have remained faithful to the old traditions and provided a fine lesson for the younger generation as to the proper method of fighting out a golfing duel in the grand manner". The first 36 holes were close, with Sayers leaving Sunningdale with a one-hole advantage, and he outplayed Kirkaldy at Walton Heath, to win the match by a score of 6 and 5. In many ways the present seniors' tour is a direct descendant of this small event.

The last big challenge match before the war came in June 1913, when Ray and Duncan halved a £100-a-side match at Walton Heath and Sunningdale.

These matches, though representing but a fraction of those played, were viewed by contemporaries as the most important exhibitions of the time. As today, when there was big money at stake, who ever put up the money, the public and the players sat up and took notice.

NOTES
1. *Golf Illustrated*, December 4th, 1908
2. *Golf*, April 22nd, 1895
3. *Golf*, September 24, 1897
4. *Golf Illustrated*, November 7th, 1902
5. *Golf Illustrated*, June 23, 1905
6. *Golf Illustrated*, September 5th, 1905
7. *Golf Illustrated*, October 19th, 1906
8. *Golf Illustrated*, November 16th, 1906
9. *Golf Illustrated*, December 21st, 1906
10. *Golf Illustrated*, August 2nd, 1907
11. *Golf Illustrated*, May 7th, 1909

5. International Tours and Matches Abroad

The ball that Harry Vardon went to the U.S.A. to promote in 1900.

There were two types of international golf events played in this period. Those where the players went abroad and those where they never left Britain.

U.S.A. Tours

One very attractive option for a professional seeking to better himself was to emigrate to America. Many did. At the same time there was a number of tours there by leading players who duly returned to Britain – as are now discussed.

Three tours for the price of two – Vardon and Taylor in 1900

In 1900 Vardon was engaged by A.G. Spalding, a well-known American sporting goods manufacturer to tour America with the purpose of promoting the new Spalding "Vardon Flyer" golf ball. The tour was managed by Charles Cox of Spalding. It was rumoured that Vardon had received a four-year contract from Spalding, at £800 per annum. The tour was to be split, with Vardon playing in the States from January to May, returning to Britain in May to play in the Open, and then going back in June to the States, where he would stay until the end of the year.

From a golfing point of view the tour (both halves) was a great success. Vardon estimated that he played and won over 50 matches, halved two and lost 13. 11 of those defeats were in matches in which he had to play the best ball of at least two opponents. The only man to defeat him in singles play was Bernard Nicholls, a transplanted Englishman from Kent. Vardon attributed one of those defeats to the fact that the course at Ormond, Florida, had no grass on it, and consisted mainly of loose sand. The tour is credited with giving additional impetus to the already booming American golf game.

On the first half of his tour, what interested journalists as much as the golfing results was the amount of money Vardon was supposed to be making. Writing about his basic contract of £800 a year, a commentator in *The Pall Mall Gazette* in February 1900 defended Vardon, saying that "Vardon is more than merely a good professional. He is the best golfer that the world

73

has produced. If the number of almighty dollars that he is to receive is excessive, which we do not think, it would be right that he should receive it excessively liberally, as he golfs excessively well." In addition to his salary, Vardon seems to have been receiving £50 per exhibition. One article reported that "the Lakewood Golf Club has declined Vardon's services for an exhibition match at its tournament the last week in April, thinking his fee of $250 is too high."[1] The current exchange rate was about $5 to £1. It was estimated by one American paper that Vardon earned about $5,250 (£1,050) between January and May.

After playing in the snow at St Lawrence Harbour Golf Club, in New Jersey, Vardon headed to the warm southern climate in Florida, and then slowly worked his way back to New York. The highlights of this first tour included defeating Willie Smith at St Augustine, Florida, by 2 and 1, defeating Alexander Findlay at Palm Beach, Florida, by one hole and losing to Bernard Nicholls at Ormond, Florida. Vardon found that the warm Florida air added yards to his drives, and that the heat made it impossible to play wearing a jacket. He took to wearing a waistcoat with sleeves, which helped keep his arms together.

A breach of etiquette
Leaving Florida, he worked his way back north, and on March 31st he defeated Willie Dunn by 11 and 10 at the Hampton Roads Golf and Country Club in Virginia. A curious interpretation of course etiquette took place when Vardon was playing the best ball of two amateurs at the Palmetto Golf Club in Aiken, South Carolina. One of his opponents accused Vardon of discourtesy, because he was smoking a cigarette while playing. The opponent claimed that "we might expect as much respect as an amateur would receive on any English course."[2] Vardon was very annoyed by this remark, but did not smoke any more during the round. After the match, the rest of the members felt that Vardon had done nothing wrong, and that he was the victim of a discourtesy.

After defeating Dunn, Vardon went to Atlantic City, New Jersey, where, at the Atlantic City Country Club, he defeated the best ball of H.M. Harriman and Findlay Douglas by a score of 9 and 8. Vardon played some matches in the New York area, before returning to England on May 2nd.

He sailed back to the States on June 20th and stayed for another six months. If Vardon was receiving £50 a match and played about 65 matches, he would have earned about £3,250 from exhibitions. First prize at the US Open was $150 (£30), while he was purportedly receiving £800 from Spalding. Combined, that would take his minimum earnings to about £4,000, excluding any other prize money or sponsorship money that he might have received. Taylor admitted to making a deal worth £2,000 with an American publisher during his much shorter tour, and that did not include what he made through exhibition matches and tournament earnings. It would not be unreasonable to assume that Vardon made more than £4,000 for his longer tour.

The second half of Vardon's tour progressed in much the same manner as

George Lyon.

the first half, and included stops in Michigan, Colorado, Connecticut, Massachusetts, Maine, New York, New Jersey and Canada. Vardon played a match on average every other day, but many were on courses attached to hotels that did not offer a fair test of any player's ability. It was reckoned that the hardest test took place at Morristown, New Jersey, on September 20th, when Vardon played the best ball of George Low, the runner-up in the US Open the previous year, and Tom Hutchison. The pair beat him by 10 and 9. Unshaken, Vardon then headed for Canada, arriving in Toronto the next day. On September 23rd he took on the best ball of George Lyon and Vere Brown over the Rosedale Course, and won by 5 and 4. He then went to Montreal and played two matches at the Royal Montreal Golf Club. In the morning he lost to the best ball of two professionals, George Cumming, of Toronto Golf Club, and Tom Smith, the home pro. In the afternoon he broke the course record, in defeating the best ball of two amateurs, Percy Taylor and Gordon Macdougall. He then moved on to Wheaton, Illinois, for the US Open, which was played on October 4th and 5th.

Meanwhile, on August 4th, J.H. Taylor set sail on his own American expedition to promote his club-making business in the States. His partner,

75

George Cann, was based in Pittsburgh. He left England without any pre-arranged programme except that he intended to play in the US Open in October. When he landed in New York, he and Cann met with Colonel Harvey of the publishers Harper & Bros. who offered the champion a contract of £2,000 a year to write articles about golf, and offered to manage his subsequent tour. Taylor, for whom this was his "first introduction to the possibility of earning big money in a very pleasant manner", immediately accepted the offer.

The press were all clamouring for a meeting between Vardon and Taylor, and it was reported in the September 14th *Golf Illustrated* that "Vardon's manager, Mr. C.S. Cox of Spalding and Co., has tried very hard to induce Taylor's manager to arrange a match or series of matches forthwith . . . but Messrs Harper's representative, Mr. G.S. Coxe, who is looking after Taylor's interests, not unnaturally thinks it would be no fair test of the merits of the two men if they were to meet now."

Vardon *versus* Taylor?
Much was written about the failure of the players to oppose one another. By October, the New York journal *Outing* wrote, "if the two English Professionals do not meet in a match before [the US Open at] Chicago, it will not be for lack of effort making on the part of some newspaper reporters and the American manager of the English ex-champion [Vardon]. There appears to be a concerted effort among these to literally hound Taylor into a match, which is not pleasing in the eyes of sportsmen, since the avowed purpose is the size of the purse attainable." Taylor mentioned the press campaign in his autobiography, *Golf: My Life's Work,* but offered no explanation as to why they never met in an exhibition match. Vardon made no mention of the issue in either *The Complete Golfer* or *My Golfing Life*. The two men had met in exhibition singles matches seven times in Britain between 1894 and 1899, and each had won three and one was halved. The reasons for their not playing in the States must have been financial.

Taylor, who had not been feeling well since his arrival in America, had a less strenuous tour than Vardon. In September, after resting at Ashbury Park, New Jersey, he played over the Deal golf course – perhaps the name made him feel more at home – and lost a best ball match to the local professionals. On September 15th he played at the Myopia Hunt Club, near Boston, before taking on Joe Lloyd and John Dingwell at the Essex County Club on September 19th. The next day he played at the Brookline Country Club, against the best ball of the local professionals in the morning, and that of two amateurs in the afternoon.

Both visitors competed in the US Open, which Vardon duly won, with Taylor finishing second, two shots behind. Vardon finished his tour, mainly in the north-eastern states, and returned home in December.

Taylor, however, was tempted to stay in America. Colonel Harvey and his friends were prepared to provide the capital for a new club-making company called J.H. Taylor & Cann, if Taylor remained in America. He

The Cann and Taylor stamp.

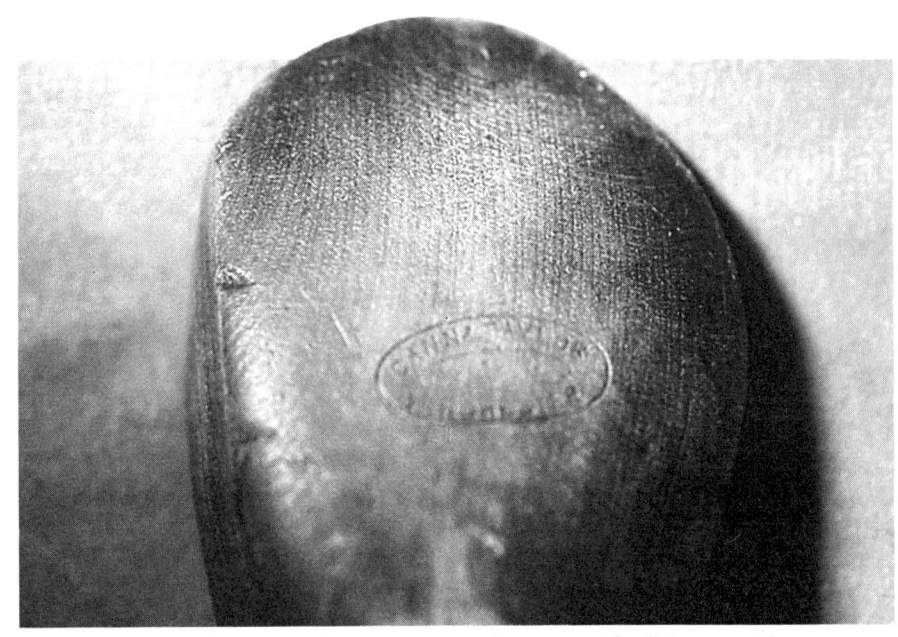

actually went as far as to sign a contract, but his wife did not wish to move to America, and Mid-Surrey Golf Club were not prepared to grant him a 12-month leave of absence; so he exercised his opt-out clause and returned home.

A short trip to Mexico

In late 1905, Bernard Nicholls arrived in Britain "with a special commission from the president of the Mexico Country Club, to recruit players for a golfing extravaganza in San Pedro de los Pinos that would include an open championship and an international match in January 1906." The object of the exercise was to popularise the Mexico Country Club in the winter season with Americans from across the border.

Nicholls offered invitations to Braid, Taylor, Harry Vardon and Tom Vardon, but they all declined. The four who accepted were Andrew Kirkaldy, Sandy Herd, Jack White and Rowland Jones. They sailed to New York, and then travelled by a special train down to San Pedro. Willie Smith was the local professional at the Mexico Country Club, and won the stroke play competition easily by 12 strokes. The British players were affected by the heat and travel. Rowland Jones suffered from blistered feet caused by playing in rubber shoes, "when I should have done better to have stuck to my nail shoes". Worst of all were the putting greens, which were sand, and made approaching and putting difficult for the visitors.

There was then a team competition of American-based professionals (most of whom were Scottish by birth) versus the British players. The Americans won. Jones, Kirkaldy and Herd all played their way back to New York through the southern states. Jones described the tour as "strenuous work – hours together in the train, and then having to tumble out and play first class golf". All of them lost to Walter Travis at Palm Beach, Florida, at one of their stops. The four British players were back home by the end of February. It was an exhausting, but lucrative, trip.

Duncan's American tour
In the autumn of 1911, George Duncan undertook a six-week tour of America, thus missing the *News of the World* Tournament finals, for which he had previously qualified. He was based at the Deal Beach Golf Club, in New Jersey, and played in Philadelphia, Boston, New York, Chicago and "several other places". The report in the October 13th *Golf Illustrated* commented that Duncan's individual performances had been excellent, but he did not "appear to be fortunate in his partners in the four ball matches". He did succeed in winning the Open Championship of Pennsylvania in a field that included future Open Champion, Jock Hutchison, and the leading amateur, Chick Evans.

For one of his matches, Duncan had an Indian, known as "Big Chief Scratch Golf", for a caddie. Their only means of communication was by grunts. The Indian would grunt once for a bad shot and twice for a good one, and Duncan responded with the same. He claimed "we built up a system that was effective as any bush telegraph." Upon his return, he felt that "the American experience did me a world of good. The following year I won the Belgian Open and a tournament [called] the Championship of Lucerne."

Ted and Harry's lucrative journey
In 1913 Vardon returned for another tour of America, this time with Ted Ray. It lasted from August until November, and was sponsored by Lord Northcliffe, then proprietor of the *Daily Mail*. This trip, and especially the US Open, have been written about extensively. I will comment on only two aspects – travel and money – and then only from the perspective of how they were reported in Britain. As with the 1900 tour, money issues were almost as important as the golf itself, and had raised their head even before the duo had set sail. On June 20th, *Golf Illustrated* published a report that Ray and Vardon would each receive £200 for playing in an exhibition match in San Francisco. Money dominated the report of their first major tournament, at the Shawnee Golf Club. The total purse for the event was £150, but "Vardon and Ray are stated to have received £200 from the proprietor of the course."[3] Appearance money in addition to prize money is obviously not simply a product of the age of television.

Their policy of charging high fees was defended by *Golf Illustrated*: "A considerable volume of hot air seems to have been expended on the fact that Vardon and Ray are asking four hundred dollars [£80] for exhibition matches . . . The two men cannot be expected to spend the bulk of their time in the States playing exhibition matches for the same fees that they obtain at home . . . [They] stand right at the top of their business, and like other highly paid experts, they are entitled to exceptional remuneration. Summed up, their attitude – and a very logical one it seems to us – is this: 'we are not particularly anxious to play a lot of exhibition matches, but we are willing to do so if we are paid what we consider the value of our service.'"[4] A.W. Tillinghast wrote that: "He and Ray had their price for participating in exhibitions, and if the clubs did not wish to engage them,

Chick Evans.

A.W. Tillinghast.

there was no compulsion about it. As a matter of fact, while they were with us, the wires were hot with offers from every section. It is Vardon's business to play for hire, and to teach golf and comment for money."[5] Vardon and Ray's attitude to exhibition matches would not be out of place in sports today.

The tour itself was quite gruelling, covering coast-to-coast and Canada. They played 41 fourball matches, winning 40, but their schedule was so crammed that they were not able to play another 32 matches that had been

79

booked. The travel took its toll on Vardon, and he was no doubt feeling the difference between taking on a protracted tour when he was 29 years of age, and attempting a similar task when the wrong side of 40. "As a man grows older his muscles generally lose a little of their recuperative power."[6] It was reported that the two men travelled a total of 35,000 miles in about three months. They seemed to live on trains and boats, sleeping on average only one night a week in a hotel.[7] If they did receive $400 a match, they would have earned at least $16,400 (£3,280) between them, excluding prize money.

European tours

Golf was gradually becoming more popular in Europe during this period, especially in France. According to the 1894/95 *Golfing Annual,* there were eleven golf clubs (plus two ladies' clubs) in France, three in Holland, two each in Belgium and Switzerland, and one each in Spain and Italy. By 1902 there were 21 golf clubs in France. This had increased to 30 by 1907, and 42 by 1909. In Germany there were five golf clubs in 1902, 15 in 1907 and 19 in 1910. The number in Belgium was constant – eight. There were five clubs in Italy in 1902, doubling to ten in 1910. It is therefore not surprising to find the British-based professionals playing more and more exhibitions and tournaments in Europe. Many of the exhibition matches were played in conjunction with tournaments, some of which will be discussed in detail later.

In the winter of 1896, Vardon, Taylor, Herd, Archie Simpson and Willie Auchterlonie were invited to play a series of exhibitions at Pau, along with the local professional, Joe Lloyd, to celebrate the club's 50th anniversary. Vardon, being from Jersey, spoke some French, and was put in charge of the financial matters of the party. Unfortunately he didn't actually speak much French, and became easily confused when dealing with ticket collectors and other minor matters. Fortunately they were met at Bordeaux by Lloyd, who took over the translating duties. They proceeded to play one event on February 24th and 25th, and then a 72-hole tournament on March 1st and 2nd. The matches on the 24th and 25th were "an American style tournament", which was a round robin where all the players played one another. Taylor, Auchterlonie, Simpson and Vardon won three matches each, and split the first prize.

J.H. Taylor made his first visit to Cannes in February 1905, on his way back from Varenna, where he had been laying out a course. Upon his arrival he was welcomed by the Grand Duke Michael of Russia, General Arthur Paget, Lord Wolverton "and other habitués of the Côte d'Azur". He immediately embarked on a week of fairly hectic social golf, in which he and the local professionals, Freemantle and Callaway, partnered the cream of society in a series of matches. On the last day, Taylor played an exhibition match against the best ball of Freemantle and Callaway, and still won by a score of 6 and 5.

In October the same year, Tom Vardon and Albert Tingey accompanied a group of amateurs to Paris. After the amateur team match, the two professionals took on Massy and Louis Tellier in a fourball foursome, and lost by 3 and 2. The next day, Massy defeated Vardon, but Tingey overcame Tellier.

In August 1906 Taylor was in Switzerland, and halved a match with Massy at the Engadine Club, in Samaden; then in early 1907 found himself in Egypt. He had been recommended by A.J. Balfour to design a course at Heliopolis, and staked out the greens and fairways in three days. Back in Cairo, he played an exhibition match for a purse of £26.25, with the winner receiving £16.80, against W.H. Fulford, who was the local professional at Helouan. From Egypt he sailed to France where he joined Braid, Harry Vardon, Tom Vardon, Herd, Massy, Sayers, White and Ray in Cannes for "by far the most important golfing event that has yet taken place on the Continent".

The whole event was organised by Grand Duke Michael of Russia and the Cannes Golf Club. The tournament carried £150 in prize money and £150 in expenses. Arnaud Massy was the only French representative, and pulled off a major upset by winning the stroke play event and the four-ball foursome event in partnership with Jones. The British players then headed home via Hyères, where they played two foursomes matches in the morning and a stroke play competition in the afternoon.

In 1908 Vardon, Braid and Taylor went back to France for a series of events. The main one was a two-day meeting in Nice, on March 17th and 18th. On the first day Vardon won the stroke play tournament (and £42.50), with Massy coming second by four shots. Braid and Gassiat were tied for third. The next morning was a four-ball stroke play foursome, which ended in a tie between Massy and Callaway (the local professional) and Braid and Gassiat. That afternoon therewas a singles match play event, pitting the British against the French. Braid, Taylor and Vardon all emerged victorious against Massy, Gassiat and Bomboudiac respectively. Working their way back to England, Taylor won a 36-hole stroke play tournament at Hyères; Braid was second and Vardon third. Massy and Gassiat finished 11 and 14 strokes behind. Vardon then came first at Costebelle, winning another £20, and Massy was second, four shots back.

In 1910 Taylor was invited to Rome, and on March 16th played in a pro-am foursome, and on the 17th played an exhibition match against the local professional, Robert Doig. The local suffered badly from nerves, and lost by 22 strokes over 36 holes. At the same time, Vardon, who was on holiday in Le Touquet, went to visit Switzerland, and played an exhibition match at Montreux against the local professional, T. Nolan, winning by a score of 3 and 2.

On July 29th two foursomes were played after the tournament to celebrate the opening of the new course at Lombartzyde, in Belgium. Braid and Willie Park defeated Herd and Charles, another unfortunate local professional, while Vardon and John Park halved their match with Taylor and Ray.

A month later Braid and Vardon were back in France, where they lost two foursomes matches to Massy and Lafitte on the 22nd and 23rd of August. Taylor went to France again in November. He played and split two matches with Jean Gassiat on the 13th and 14th of the month.

On February 18th, 1911, Ben Sayers, who was spending the winter as the professional in Monte Carlo, played F. Philips, the professional at Mentone, for a purse of £20, and won by a score of 4 and 2.

France and Italy

In March 1911 Braid, Taylor, Sherlock and Massy went on another major tour of France and Italy, playing in St Jean de Luz, Costebelle, Nice and Rome. At St Jean on March 28th, the four played a mini tournament over 72 holes, which resulted in a tie between Massy and Taylor, who split the first prize of £45. Braid won £10 for coming third and Sherlock £5 for finishing last. The foursomes match was postponed for a day because of bad weather, and was halved the following day, the 30th. On April 1st they moved on to the Costebelle course, at Hyères, where Braid won the mini tournament. Taylor and Sherlock finished tied for second, and Massy was last. On the 2nd they played the Hyères course, and Braid came first again, with Massy second, Taylor third and Sherlock last. They played a foursomes match the same afternoon, Braid and Sherlock getting the better of Taylor and Massy.

They then moved on to Cagnes, where they played a 36-hole foursome match on April 4th. Braid and Sherlock won the £30 first prize, and Taylor and Massy won £10. They continued with a 36-hole mini tournament the next day, which Massy won. Crossing into Italy, they reached Rome to play a 36-hole foursome on the 7th, which was halved. On the 8th they played another mini tournament, which Braid won. There was a total of £100 prize money for the Rome events. The British players then returned home.

Accounts of this tour give some insight into travel conditions of the time. In a report in the *News of the World* it was estimated that Braid, Taylor and Sherlock had travelled over 3,000 miles, spending four nights on trains, in order to play in five tournaments. In a record that any modern airline could be proud of, the quartet lost their luggage four times. At Costebelle, they all had to play in borrowed clothing. On the journey between Nice and Rome, which ended up taking 22 hours, their train broke down, and they had to walk two miles to the nearest station, carrying their baggage. The report says that "during the trudge Massy could be heard volubly decrying in most vigorous French the shortcomings of Italian railways, and again, in his best English, to enliven his colleagues, describing and suggesting what Andrew Kirkaldy would say and do if similarly placed."

Had they travelled with him back to St Jean de Luz in 1912, they might have had the opportunity to find out. As it was, Kirkaldy finished second in a mini tournament, six shots behind Massy, on February 20th. That afternoon, the large Scot teamed with the big Frenchman to defeat Lafitte and Dauge in the foursomes event. Five days later Braid (as usual) defeated the local professional, B. Cockburn, by a score of 3 and 1 at Le Touquet.

In 1912, the Triumvirate made another trip to the South of France, to take part in a tournament to mark the opening of the Monte Carlo links. Massy finished first, Vardon second and Braid tied for third with Gassiat.

A mini tournament between the top four finishers, with a purse of £50, was held at the close of the 1913 Belgian Open. Unusually for a mini tournament, the format was a knock-out competition. Braid defeated Rowland Jones and then the new Belgian champion, Tom Ball. First prize was £25.

In February 1914, Duncan played Herd in a two-day match in Cannes and Nice, with Herd winning. Duncan went on to play Gassiat in Chantilly, and easily defeated the Frenchman.

These tours to Europe were generally very strenuous, but also very lucrative, according to the known details of the prize money. Taken in conjunction with the development of major national open championships in France, Belgium and, briefly but controversially Germany, they reflect the increase in popularity of golf in Europe and the popularity of the leading British professionals amongst Europeans.

International Matches

The PGA England *versus* Scotland International

In direct contrast to the strenuous excursions abroad were the international team matches where everybody stayed at home. These, of course, were mainly the matches between English and Scottish professionals. The England-Scotland fixture was born at the Annual General Meeting of the PGA on December 8th, 1902, when W.C. Gaudin proposed that an international match should be held between the English and Scottish professionals during the Open Championship week. Jack White seconded the motion, and it was "unanimously recommended to the committee to be dealt with". A month later, at the January 19th PGA Committee Meeting, it was announced that "the Prestwick Golf Club had most kindly granted the committee permission to play a professional England *v* Scotland match on their links on Monday, June 8th [two days prior to the Open Championship] and it was decided that only members of the Association should be eligible to take part". At the March 23rd Committee Meeting it was agreed that the qualification would be by birth, that the teams would have 12 players each, and the format would be match play. Sandy Herd was appointed the Scottish captain and Harry Vardon the English.

The teams were duly selected, and a week before the match it was announced that there would be singles play in the morning and foursomes in the afternoon. The first English team consisted of Harry Vardon, J.H. Taylor, Tom Vardon, Ted Ray, Rowland Jones, Peter Rainford, James Sherlock, Fred Collins, Tom Renouf, Albert Tingey, Walter Toogood and Jack Rowe. The Scottish team was James Braid, Sandy Herd, Jack White, James Kinnell, Willie Park, Willie Fernie, Ben Sayers, Ralph Smith, Robert Thomson, James Hepburn, George Coburn and James Kay. It was felt that the Scottish side was unrepresentative of the best Scottish talent, because some of the leading players were not members of the PGA, and therefore not eligible to play. Indeed, the night after the match. Taylor chaired a meeting "to obviate certain misunderstandings which had arisen between the Association and some of the Scottish professionals who have hitherto stood aloof from the Association". The meeting was deemed a success by all who attended.

The match itself was an exciting affair. At the end of the singles round, the score stood at six points each (one point was awarded for a win, and no points were given for a half or a loss). Harry Vardon defeated Braid, and Taylor beat Herd, in the leading singles matches. However the Scottish pair got their revenge in the afternoon, winning their foursomes match by a hole. White and Kinnell beat Tom Vardon and Ray, and the veterans Park and Fernie defeated Jones and Rainford. This left Scotland three up with three to play. But the English team staged a comeback, with Sherlock and Collins defeating Sayers and Smith, and Renouf and Tingey beating Thomson and Hepburn. Scotland now led by one match, with one match still to be completed. Coburn and Kay halved it with the English pair of Toogood and Rowe, and Scotland won the match by 15 points to 14.

The 1904 match was played on June 4th at Sandwich. Scotland took a two-point lead in the singles, but the English team again came back in the foursomes, and, with only one match still on the course, England were leading by eight points to seven. The remaining Scottish pair, the veterans

The English team, 1903: (standing) Sherlock, Collins, Rowe, H. Vardon, Jones, Rainford, (seated) Toogood, Renouf, Taylor, T. Vardon, Ray, Tingey.

Scotland: (standing) Smith, Coburn, Braid, Thomson, Park, Fernie, (seated) Kinnell, Kay, Herd, White, Sayers, Hepburn. The team included five Open champions.

Kirkaldy and Sayers, proved too strong for Jones and Sherlock, and won by two holes. Thus the overall match ended in a tie, with both teams on eight points.

In an attempt to provide more interest for the spectators in the foursomes, the combinations of Vardon and Taylor and Braid and Herd were broken up, and the first three played with partners of "less repute", namely Ernest Gray, Tom Williamson and Ralph Smith respectively. Herd was paired with Willie Fernie.

The 1905 international

The 1905 match was even more exciting than the 1904 one. This time the English team held a one-point advantage after the singles. In the foursomes, the experiment of the previous year was not repeated, and the leading players were partnered. The match between Taylor and Vardon and Herd and Braid was halved when Vardon holed a five-yard putt on the last hole. White and Park and Sayers and Kirkaldy both won their matches, to put Scotland up by a point. The next two matches were halved, so once again it came down to the last foursome of Tingey and P.J. Gaudin against Kinnell and George Coburn. Coming to the 18th and final hole, this match was square. Kinnell underhit his approach to the green, and Coburn overhit his. Kinnell put his next shot within four feet of the hole, but Tingey, with a stroke in hand, holed his putt to win the game. So the overall match

The English team:
(standing)
A.H. Toogood,
J. Sherlock,
E. Ray, T. Williamson,
T.G. Renouf, H. Vardon,
E. Gray; (seated)
P.J. Gaudin, T. Vardon,
J.H. Taylor, A Tingey,
R. Jones.

The Scottish team:
(standing) T. Yeoman,
W. Park, A. Kirkaldy,
J. Braid, R. Thomson,
A. Herd; (seated)
B. Sayers, J. Kinnell,
J. White, G. Coburn,
J. Hepburn, J. Kirkaldy.

ended in another tie, with both teams on seven points.

Things did not go well for Scotland in the 1906 match, despite a very promising start in the singles, when Braid beat Taylor and Herd defeated Vardon. Only Thomson and Sayers were able to win their matches, and the Englishmen won the other eight to take a four-point lead. In the afternoon Taylor and Vardon triumphed over Braid and Herd by a score of 5 and 3, to give England a five-point lead with five matches remaining. When Ray and Tom Vardon then beat White and Thomson, victory belonged to England. The final score was England 12, Scotland 6.

A new match format was tried in 1907 at Hoylake, when, instead of 12 players a side playing singles and foursomes, there were two teams of 16 golfers playing singles matches over 36 holes. At the end of the first 18 holes, Scottish players were leading in 11 of the matches, English in four, and one match was even. Unfortunately things did not go well for Scotland in the afternoon. The English players won the four matches in which they were leading at the turn, and came back to win three of the matches in which they trailed. They also won the one that had been square. Thus the English team won by 8 points to 5.

The biggest comeback of the day was by George Cawsey, who had trailed Duncan by four holes after the first 18. The Englishman managed to secure a half. That match, however, was not without controversy. At the fourth hole of the second round, Duncan had a three-yard putt. He holed the putt, but it was claimed that he caused his ball to move while addressing it. Duncan denied this, but the hole was halved as a compromise. Had the ruling not gone against him, Duncan would have won the match but, in any event, it would not have affected the overall outcome.

There was a greater controversy before a single shot of the whole event had been played. Alex Smith, the reigning US Open champion, and a Scotsman by birth, was selected for the Scottish team. However he was not a member of the PGA, and had to stand down. When Massy joined the PGA a month later, a writer in the July 5th *Golf Illustrated* wondered, somewhat tongue-in-cheek, whether Massy would now be allowed to play for Scotland, as he had joined the Scottish section.

It was decided, immediately after the 1907 match had finished, to revert to the old format of singles and foursomes play. Only eight players were

The English team of 1909: (standing) R. Jones, E. Ray, T. Ball, J.H. Taylor, C.H. Mayo, J. Sherlock, (seated) H. Vardon, F. Robson, T. Williamson, T. Vardon, P.J. Gaudin.

The Scottish team, 1909: (standing) C.R. (Ralph) Smith, J. Braid, J. White, R. Thomson, B. Sayers Jnr.; (seated) B. Sayers Snr., A. Herd, G. Duncan, F. Coltart, A Kirkaldy.

chosen for both sides in the 1908 match at Prestwick, but the event had to be abandoned because of heavy and persistent rain. It was suggested that it could be played on the Monday, but it was felt this would be unfair to the players, as they would have no break before the Open Championship itself began.

The 1909 match at Deal was never close. In the singles Braid halved his match with Taylor, Duncan beat Tom Vardon, and Ralph Smith defeated P.J. Gaudin; but the other nine matches went to England. By the end of the morning, the English team had an insurmountable lead of 7 points – which made the foursomes of academic interest. These were split, with both sides gaining two points, to give England victory by 11 points to 4.

Once again Scotland got off to a promising start in the 1910 match at St Andrews, but it was not to last. Although Braid lost to Vardon, Herd halved his match with Taylor, and Duncan beat Ray. But then the rest of the morning went England's way, with only Thomson salvaging any more points for Scotland. At the end of the morning, England had a six-point lead, with six more points to play for in the afternoon. Braid and Herd gave Scotland the start she needed, by defeating Vardon and Taylor by a score of 5 and 4. But Ray and Tom Vardon defeated Duncan and Hepburn in the next match, giving England victory. The final margin was England 11 points, Scotland 5.

With the match already decided, Sayers and Kirkaldy evidently decided to entertain the crowd in their game against Robson and Renouf. At the 11th hole, Sayers put his shot so close to the bank of a bunker that Kirkaldy could not actually stand up and play the shot at the same time. The correspondent in *Golf Illustrated* goes on to say, "Meantime, the enemy's second was in the bunker beyond the green. Anxious consultation between Andrew and Ben – latter dispatched to prospect as to enemy's position, while Andrew made tentative exploration of possibilities of stance varying between lying prone and kneeling on ground outside bunker. Frantic signals from Ben intimating easy lie of enemy". Kirkaldy hit his shot, failed to lift the ball out, and fell into the bunker in the process. At the next hole Sayers put his tee shot on to the railway line, lying amongst a cluster of stones. Kirkaldy, surveying the shot, asked Sayers if he had a short-headed mashie, to which Sayers allegedly replied, "Ay, ye want my club because ye're a feart to break yer own; na, na, man, jist play awa'." At the 17th hole, watching his five-foot putt missing the hole, Sayers went into "agonised contortions" which defied description and ended with "his actually rolling on the green in despair". It is hardly surprising that Robson proceeded to miss his own putt!

A coronation match

At the PGA AGM on June 18th, 1910, "a suggestion from Royal St George's, that for next year only, the Professional International be abandoned and a Coronation Match be played instead – on the Saturday preceding the Open Championship – foursomes, nine couples a side, Amateurs *v* Professionals, was agreed to. "Accordingly a PGA side took on an amateur one at Sandwich the following June. As fore mentioned, the match was a rout, with the professionals winning easily by 8 matches to 1. One match featured Massy and Braid against John Ball and Chick Evans, a leading American amateur and future champion. Rather disappointingly, the professionals won easily by 6 and 5.

The 1912 match at Muirfield was closely contested. Each side gained five points in the morning singles, and then victories in the last two foursome matches enabled them to tie the overall match at 8 points each. Frank Kinloch reported that the crowd "seemed much more interested in the result than the players, some of whom, truth to tell, seemed to take things very easy".[8]

The 1913 Match at Hoylake was again a rout. England took a six-point lead in the morning, to secure at least a tie. Herd and Duncan raised Scottish hopes for a miracle by defeating Ray and Vardon, but, when White and Laurie Ayton could only halve their match with Taylor and Tom Ball, it was all over. The Scots failed to win another point, and England won by 13 points to 4.

There was a universal feeling that the match needed to be changed to survive. Accordingly, at the PGA AGM the same month, it was decided that instead of playing the match in tandem with the Open, it would in future be played in October, with the venue alternating between England

and Scotland. In February 1914 the PGA announced that the proprietors of *Country Life* had agreed to sponsor the event, and would be presenting a challenge cup, with gold medals for the winning team and silver ones for the losers. When war broke out in August that year, it was at first thought that the match should be played, and that proceeds from gate money could go to the Prince of Wales' Fund; but in September the idea was dropped and the match postponed indefinitely. The match was revived in 1932 and played until 1938 – but that is something for another book.

Thus the England *versus* Scotland match started off with great enthusiasm which then gradually waned. The main problem was that the English team had too much strength in depth for the Scots. After their win in 1903, the best the Scottish team could do was to tie the English on three occasions, while England were able to win five times.

The most successful English players were Rowland Jones and Tom Williamson, with 10 wins each (singles and foursomes combined). Wilfrid Reid was next, with nine wins, followed by Ray and Mayo, with eight apiece. Vardon and Taylor each had five wins. These two always drew the top Scottish players, whereas the others often played against the weaker tail. Mayo's record is noteworthy because those eight wins came in nine matches – as opposed to Ray, who played in all 17 possible. Tom Ball won six out of the eight he played, and Tom Renouf won seven out of the ten he played. On the Scottish side, the most successful player was Braid, who won eight of the 15 matches he played, while Duncan and Sayers won seven each. Herd, Park and Smith each won six.[9]

Scotland *v* Ireland

In May 1907, the Scottish section of the PGA raised a team (and provided the trophy) to play a professional Irish team at Portrush. Unlike the England *v* Scotland matches, eligibility was based on the place of employment and not birth. Alfred Toogood, then employed at Tranmore, was eligible to play for Ireland, despite being a regular member of the English team. The Scottish team was considerably weaker than those that played England because players such as Braid, Herd, Duncan and Smith were not eligible for selection under these rules. Ben Sayers and Archie Simpson played the top two matches for Scotland. Of the rest of the team, only Tom Watt was ever picked for the England match.

The match was the same format as the England match – 12 players a side, playing singles and then foursomes. The Irish team dominated the singles, winning nine matches to Scotland's two, thus securing victory before any of the foursomes had been played. The final score was Ireland 13 points to Scotland 4 points.

It was intended that the match should be played in each country alternately. However a return match was never played, so the 1907 match proved to be unique.

Other internationals

The occasional foursomes match in which two of the players were English

Ben Sayers with his caddy at North Berwick.

and two were Scottish was some times billed as an "international match". As half the leading professionals were English (Vardon, Taylor and Ray), and half were Scottish (Braid, Herd and Duncan), many exhibition matches in the period could have been advertised as "internationals". One of the more prominently covered pseudo-internationals was a match on July 24th, 1899, which was more interesting for the fact that it paired a leading professional with a leading amateur than for the nationalities of those involved. John Ball and Harry Vardon defeated Freddie Tait and Willie Park over 36 holes by 5 and 4.

More typical of this type of match was one played at Harlech in April 1903, when Braid and Herd defeated Taylor and Vardon by one hole. Two matches in 1914, one at Turnberry, and one at the Braid Hills course in Edinburgh, between Braid and Duncan and Vardon and Taylor, were described as "miniature internationals" by *Golfing*. And finally, of course, the great 1905 £400 Foursome was viewed by the press as an England *versus* Scotland match.

Although not strictly speaking relevant to any of this, the first transatlantic team match took place in France on June 30th and July 1st, 1913, when an American team played a French one. The US team, consisting of Tom McNamara, John J. McDermott, Alex Smith and Mike Brady, lost two foursomes and four singles to Arnaud Massy, Louis Tellier, Jean Gassiat and A. Lafitte, to go down to a 6-0 defeat. From this humble and humbling beginning eventually grew the transatlantic team matches of the inter-war period between the US and Great Britain.

NOTES

1. *Golf Illustrated*, April 13th 1900
2. *Golf Illustrated*, April 6th, 1900
3. *Golf Illustrated*, August 29, 1913
4. Ibid
5. *The American Cricketer*, March 1914
6. *Golf Illustrated*, November 7th, 1913
7. *Golf Illustrated*, November 28th, 1913
8. *Golf Illustrated*, June 28th, 1912
9. **Summary of International Match Results**

    1903   Scotland 15 England 14
    1904   Scotland 8 England 8
    1905   Scotland 7 England 7
    1906   England 12 Scotland 6
    1907   England 8 Scotland 5
    1908   Rain prevented play
    1909   England 11 Scotland 4
    1910   England 11 Scotland 5
    1911   Coronation Match instead
    1912   England 8 Scotland 8
    1913   England 13 Scotland 4
    1914   Cancelled because of war

6. Tournaments

Between 1894 and 1914 there were far fewer tournaments played than exhibition matches, with about one tournament being held for every three exhibitions. This period, however, saw fundamental changes in the way that tournaments were organised, the number of them and their scope. Whereas in 1894, with the exception of the Open, there were no other annual events, by 1914 the basic framework for a "tour" was in place, and the leading professionals were playing regularly in Britain, and, to a lesser extent, in Europe. Aside from the major events which attracted the leading players, a whole network of regional and district tournaments developed. As the number of tournaments increased, so did the opportunity for professionals to make a name for themselves and to earn some money in the process.

This great change can be directly attributed to the formation of the PGA. One of the association's functions was to promote tournaments for its members, and this was done very successfully. The PGA became responsible for running regional tournaments for each of their sections, as well as two national tournaments, and a tournament for assistant professionals.

The two national championships were the *News of the World* Tournament, which started in 1903, and the *Sphere* and *Tatler* cups, which began in 1911. Players qualified for these through regional tournaments, so that the *News of the World* event actually created up to nine tournaments a year, held on a regular basis. The *Sphere* and *Tatler* cups also created nine tournaments. Lesser-known players could make their mark in the qualifying events, or indeed in the finals. The PGA regional tournaments allowed players who were not quite in the top flight to compete regularly against their peers.

At a lower level than the PGA regional events were district tournaments, which gave local professionals an opportunity to test their skills against each other. At the top end of the scale, the growth of golf in Europe gave birth to Open Championships in France, Belgium and Germany, in which British professionals competed regularly.

Therefore after 1901 there grew up a regular circuit and cycle of tournaments in which the professionals could participate in direct contrast to the haphazard and random tournaments prior to that. This becomes abundantly clear after looking at the actual numbers on a yearly basis. Prior to the formation of the PGA, between 1894 and 1901, there was an average of just under 13 tournaments a year; between 1902 and 1914, this increased to nearly 31.

Prize money

The total known prize money for tournaments between 1894 and 1914 is £19,921.85, which means that the average purse was £78.43. However, the impact of the PGA, and the relative stability of the tournament schedule, is reflected in the prize money. Between 1894 and 1901, the average total purse per tournament was £55.21; after 1901, it was £89.91, an increase of 63%.

As is to be expected, £100 purses were few and far between until 1903. Aside from the Open Championship, there was only one tournament held in 1894, and one in 1895, that offered a total purse of at least £100. Including the Open, there were four tournaments that offered at least £100 in 1896, but the next year there was only the Open. This pattern then repeated itself, with two £100 purses in 1898, four in 1899 and then only one in 1900. There were then five in 1901, but only three in 1902. In 1903, the first year of the *News of the World* Tournament, only that event and the Open offered purses over £100. The situation then steadily improved, except in 1906, when only the *News of the World* and the Open topped the £100 barrier. A pre-war peak was reached in 1912, when there were ten tournaments that offered prize money in excess of £100, topped by the £500 German Open, the £400 *News of the World* and the £350 *Sphere* and *Tatler* cups. This growth was the direct result of the increasing popularity of the game, and the PGA's efforts on behalf of its members.

Although the amounts seem tiny compared with today's prizes, a successful player could earn a substantial amount by contemporary standards. In the June 12th, 1896, *Golf* it was pointed out that a total of £500 had recently been won at various tournaments, and it was "worthwhile excelling at the game". Two years later the *Dundee Courier* calculated that Vardon had won £210, Herd £140, Taylor £110 and Braid £75 in tournaments in 1898. On the other hand, as with tournament golfers today, the earnings could be very erratic from year to year. Vardon won £40 in 1897, and then shot up to £224.50 in 1898. Taylor dropped from £159 in 1904 to £60 in 1905. Braid won over £100 for three consecutive years, in 1904 dropped to 51, and then went up to £250 in 1905. Braid's earnings that year and Vardon's in 1898 were the only two occasions when a player won more than £200 in a year in tournaments in Britain and Europe. Braid and Herd both won more than £100 six times, and Vardon and Taylor four times each.

In any event, very few players consistently won money in tournaments. In his book *Taylor on Golf*, J.H. Taylor calculated that it cost a player £10 in expenses to compete in the Open, and that only the first three prizes were worth winning. A piece in *Golf Illustrated* in 1903 pointed out that, whereas the leading players were winning a lot of money in tournaments, the rank and file were not: "And what of the smaller men, those who are just second and third rate players? They have to depend not upon their prowess with the club, but upon the profits drawn from their workshops."[1]

Tournaments came in all shapes and sizes, and underwent a profound structural change after the formation of the PGA. The amount of prize money on offer was directly linked to the type of tournament which was being played.

Because many of the new tournaments were regional in nature, there was not a dramatic increase in the number of tournaments played in by the leading players, simply because they were not eligible for many of them. The most tournaments Vardon played in a year was 12, in 1898. Taylor also played in 12 that year, and then equalled that number in 1908. Braid played in a peak of 11 tournaments in 1898 and 1902. Herd played in 12 in 1898, and the most after that was 11 in 1903. Even Duncan and Ray, who set new stamina records for exhibition matches played, did not exceed 11 tournaments a year. For the whole period, Vardon, Taylor, Braid and Herd each averaged between seven and eight tournaments year and made some money doing so.

Types of tournament

Aside from the Open Championship, there was no structure to tournaments prior to the founding of the PGA. Just over 75% of the tournaments played between 1894 and 1901 were organised by independent promoters – clubs, companies or individuals. These had a tendency to be played at random, sometimes in connection with a club event, or because the Open Championship was being played in the area and the leading players were already in the vicinity. The first PGA tournaments were played in 1902, and these soon totally changed the nature of tournament golf in Britain.

From 1902 to 1914, just over half of all tournaments played were sanctioned by the PGA at national and regional level, compared with only about 20% promoted by clubs or individuals. At the same time there was a growth of tournaments organised at district levels by local associations. However the backbone of tournament schedules from 1902 onwards was the PGA, with both regional and national tournaments. It is important to understand the nature and qualification requirements of the different types of tournament.

Open championships

Until 1906, the Open Championship was the only major national open tournament in which British players participated regularly. Vardon and Taylor both played in the 1900 US Open Championship, and Vardon, Ray and Wilfrid Reid all played in the 1913 US Open. However, trips to America were exceptional events.

Trips to Europe to compete in foreign Opens became commonplace after 1906. A British contingent was present at the first French Open held in 1906, and at each later one. The Belgian Open was first held in 1910, and leading British players took part in it each year up to 1914. The "German" Open was played in 1911 and 1912, with a field full of British players. As today, the British Open Championship was the single most important tournament of the year. Although the foreign Opens could be lucrative in terms of prize money, they lacked the prestige of the British event.

Independent tournaments

A study of independent tournaments with a total purse of at least £100 shows how irregular they were. The Musselburgh Open Tournament, which was held seven times between 1895 and 1906 (and nine times in total), sums up the random nature of the independent tournaments. It was held the most frequently of any independent tournament in the period, but was not a set fixture. The avowed intention was that it would be played when the Open was in Scotland. Each of the seven times it was played, the Open was in Scotland, but it was not played in 1905, when the Open was held in St Andrews. The prize money fluctuated between £41 and £100, with no set pattern.

Another big independent tournament held at Cruden Bay. It was played four times, in 1899, 1909, 1911 and 1914, with no apparent rationale for deciding when the event took place. On the first three occasions the Open was held in England, and on the last it was in Scotland. It was played once in April, once in May and twice in June. The prize money was consistently high: £120 in 1899, and £150 in 1909, 1911 and 1914.

The four major tournaments at North Berwick again show the mercurial nature of these types of events. Taking place in 1895, 1896, 1908 and 1909, the first three were held to coincide with the Open Championship in Scotland. But the pattern was broken in 1909, when the Open was at Deal. The total purse in 1895 was £75, but fell to £51 the next year. In 1908 the prize money went up to £100, and in 1909 £320, at that time the largest purse offered in a tournament.

Three tournaments were held at Bushey Hall in 1898, 1902 and 1905, and saw dramatic increases in the prize money offered. In the first year the total purse was £24; it rose to £75 in 1902, and £260 in 1905. James Braid won all three tournaments, and saw his winnings increase from £10 to £40 to £100.

Seven other tournaments which offered a total purse of £100 or more were played on more than one occasion. These were at Montrose (1896, 1905), County Down (1896, 1898), Lytham (1898, 1905), Mid-Surrey (1899, 1901), Portmarnock (1899, 1910), Edzell (1902, 1904) and Blackpool (1907, 1908). Thus the professionals could never count on any independent tournament being played more than once, and even then there could be very long intervals between events.

The precarious nature of independent tournaments is clearly seen in one held at Bramshot. The Gordon Watney Challenge Cup, with a total purse of £80, was played there in 1910 and 1911. Then in March 1912 the club, its members having taken over ownership from the original developer, could no longer guarantee the prize money, so the tournament ceased to exist.

The *News of the World* Cup.

Regional tournaments

The first body to hold regular regional tournaments was the Midlands Golf Association, beginning in 1897. Once the PGA was formed, each of its three big sections, of which the Midlands became one, started to hold tournaments on an annual basis. The Southern Section began playing for the Tooting Bec Cup in 1901; the Northern Section held its first tournament in 1902, and the two Midland tournaments – the Chance Cup and the Challenge Cup – continued to be played along with other events. In all there were at least 88 regional events between 1897 and 1914.

However, it should be pointed out that some of these regional tournaments were also qualifying tournaments for the *News of the World* Tournament, and the *Sphere* and *Tatler* cups. For example the Midland Challenge Cup was also usually the qualifying tournament for the *News of the World* up to 1910, when it became the qualifying tournament for the *Sphere* and *Tatler* cups. This could lead to some complex results. In 1903 there were five qualifying places available, and S. Whiting finished fourth. However he was not eligible to qualify from the Midlands, and so J. Clucas, who had finished sixth, qualified instead. In 1909 Mayo and Reid both played in the Challenge Cup and finished first and second, but again were not eligible to qualify from the Midlands, and nor were A.E. Reid or A.W. Butchart, who finished fourth and fifth. The actual qualifiers for the *News of the World* cup finished third, sixth, seventh and ninth respectively.

The Northern section's Leeds Cup was often used for the *News of the World* qualifying tournament up to 1910, and afterwards the *Sphere* and *Tatler* cups. The Tooting Bec Cup was an important tournament in its own right until 1910. The death of King Edward VII caused the 1910 event to be postponed, and it was played later in the year, as part of the *News of the World* qualifying tournament, and subsequently the *Sphere* and *Tatler* cups qualifying tournaments. The complex London Foursomes tournament started as an independent event, and then became a PGA event for the last two years that it was played.

National championships

A national championship was started by the Welsh Golf Union in 1904, and the Scottish and Irish Unions followed in 1907. These were then played annually. The Welsh Championship was also the *News of the World* qualifying tournament in 1907, the players receiving prize money from both the Welsh Union and the PGA. In 1911 three events were rolled into one tournament: the Welsh Championship, the *News of the World* qualifying tournament and the Perrier Assistants qualifying tournament. These tournaments were based on a residence qualification. Thus Braid and Herd, who both worked in England, were not eligible to participate in the Scottish Championship. The growth of these national championships was not universally popular. The writer of an irate piece in *Golf Illustrated* in 1906 complained that "the proposed Scottish Professional Championship seems an altogether unnecessary addition to the calendar of events . . . It is really getting quite impossible to remember all the golf championships."[3]

District tournaments

District tournaments were first reported as such in 1896, when the Yorkshire Union of Golf Clubs held a tournament on August 18th. Regular tournaments were held by the Sussex Golfing Union and the Hampshire, Isle of Wight and Channel Islands Association, starting in 1900. By 1913 there was activity at district level across the country. Manchester was a hive of activity. The Manchester Open Tournament was held every year between 1901 and 1908, and then again in 1910, and offered a total purse of up to £75, but more usually around £45. The *Manchester Courier* Cup was played for annually, starting in 1907. In all, there were 17 local tournaments held in Manchester between 1899 and 1913.

Tournaments in Europe

Aside from the national Opens, most of the tournaments that the leading British professionals played in Europe tended to be small invitation events. Of the 18 non-Open tournaments played in Europe between 1896 and 1914, only three had more than 13 participants. British professionals were eligible to play in the 15 Opens played in France, Belgium and Germany.

Tournament formats

Between 1894 and 1914, 79% of the tournaments were the stroke play format which dominates modern golf, and 8% were match play. The remaining 13% were a combined format of both stroke play and match play, virtually never seen in the professional game today, but a form of which is used for the Amateur Championship. Whereas the match play tournaments represented a small percentage of the total, they included two of the most important events of the year. Both the *News of the World* Tournament and the *Sphere* and *Tatler* cups finals were decided by match play, the latter being a foursomes tournament.

The combined format was a combination of stroke play and match play. Usually there was a day of stroke play, and the leaders then qualified for the match play eliminations, sometimes as many as 16, or as few as four. This format seems to have first become popular in 1896. A description of the format in *Golf Illustrated* on May 22nd, 1896, referred to it as "the new system of two competitions – the first by strokes and the second by holes". It was a particularly favoured form of competition in the big independent tournaments. It was used at County Down in 1896 and 1898, Montrose in 1896 and 1905, Lytham in 1898 and 1905, Mid-Surrey in 1899 and 1901, Portmarnock in 1899 and 1910, Edzell in 1902 and 1904, Bushey Hall in 1902 (but not the other two Bushey Hall tournaments), Blackpool in 1907 and 1908, all four Cruden Bay events (1899, 1909, 1911, 1914), and at Musselburgh in 1896 and 1901, but not the other times. In all, it was the tournament format on 65 occasions. The total prize money was over £50 37 times and over £100 on 23 of those occasions. In all, the popularity of this format can be seen by the fact that, where the prize money is known, it averaged £87.14, compared with the overall prize money average of £78.43. Such an event was normally played over three days, and had a wider and more complicated prize money distribution than ordinary stroke play tournaments. The average number of prizes for stroke play tournaments, where it is known, was eight. In the combined format it was 12. Prizes were given in the stroke play segment, and then larger prizes for the match play part.

For example, at the 1901 Musselburgh Tournament, Braid, Kirkaldy, Herd and Taylor finished with the best four scores in the medal round, and then played two rounds of direct elimination match play, for prizes of £25, £20, £15 and £10. Meanwhile the players who had finished fifth to twelfth in the stroke play received prizes of £5, £3.50, £1.50 and £1, depending on their placing.

The 1904 Edzell Tournament had a more complex system of prize distribution. The top 12 finishers in the stroke play all received prize money ranging from £9.50 to £1. The top eight also qualified for the direct elimination match play phase. Vardon finished joint first in the stroke play, and won £9.50. Braid finished joint third, and won £6.33. They both then went on to reach the final of the match play tournament, where Braid defeated Vardon. Braid received £20 for this, bringing his total winnings in the tournament to £26.33. Vardon won another £15, bringing his total to £24.50.

The prize money at the 1904 Walton Heath Tournament, held on June 11th to June 14th, was dispensed in a similar fashion. According to the official notification of the tournament in *Golf Illustrated*: "Prizes to the amount of £105 will be given. On the 11th [of June] competitors will play 36 holes medal play when £5 will be given for the best first round of 18 holes and £5 for the best second round of 18 holes. The first 8 scorers will play off on the 13th and 14th by match play for prizes of £25, £15, two of £10 and four of £5. There will be four prizes of £3 and four of £2 on the 11th for the best scores over 36 holes after the first eight."

It was also a popular format at district level, when its use was first recorded in 1900. Between 1900 and 1914, 20 district level tournaments out of 55 played used this format. The average prize money for these events was £20.88p. Again, the prize money was widely spread, with an average of 12 players benefiting.

The sudden plethora of foursomes tournaments, starting in 1906, was probably a direct result of the popularity of the great 1905 £400 foursomes match. A London Pro-Am Foursomes tournament was held in 1906, and then in 1907 it split along class lines, and the London Professionals Foursomes tournament began, rapidly followed by the Midland Professionals Foursomes and Yorkshire Professionals Foursomes tournaments, in 1907 and 1909 respectively. In 1911 came the biggest foursomes tournament of them all, the *Sphere* and *Tatler* cups. In all 28 foursomes tournaments were played between 1906 and 1914.

Thus by 1914 there was a wide range of tournaments in which professionals of varying degrees of skill could participate regularly. For the leading players, these were the Open Championship, the foreign national Opens, the major PGA tournaments such as the *News of the World*, the *Sphere* and

Opposite: J.H. Taylor, James Braid and Harry Vardon, in a Clement Fowler painting, 1913.

Tatler cups and the important independent tournaments. The lesser players could all enter the Open and the major PGA events, plus the regional PGA events and the district tournaments. It was this increased opportunity for professionals at all levels that was the significant change during the period.

As has already been seen, although the amount of prize money increased steadily, a player had to win consistently to earn a good living from tournaments. However success in the major tournaments, especially the Open, brought regular exhibition matches, and invitations to tours abroad. Success at regional or district level could lead to a better club job within the area.

The Triumvirate

Vardon, Taylor and Braid played in the same event 102 times. One of the three won the event on 66 occasions, or 64.7% of the time. This shows their overall dominance. Of those 66 tournaments, Vardon won 30 (45.5%), Braid 20 (30.3%) and Taylor 16 (24.2%). In tournament play, Vardon was much superior to the other two when they were in direct competition.

Such was the domination of the Triumvirate around the turn of the century, that in September 1903 it was suggested that professional tournaments, with the exception of the Open, should be played under handicap. It was argued in 1903 in *Golf Illustrated,* "that handicap tournaments and matches would be fairer to the rank and file of the profession . . . At present the lesser lights have to content themselves with very small sums, often not sufficient to cover out of pocket expenses, while the big prizes go with somewhat monotonous regularity to one of three or four men."[2] The issue was discussed at a PGA meeting in November of the same year, and a contingency plan drawn up in the event of handicapping being introduced. No professional would have a handicap, but the leading players would carry

Lombartzyde 1910:
J. Braid, J.H. Taylor,
J. Park, A. Herd,
H. Vardon, G. Charles,
E. Ray and Willie Park.

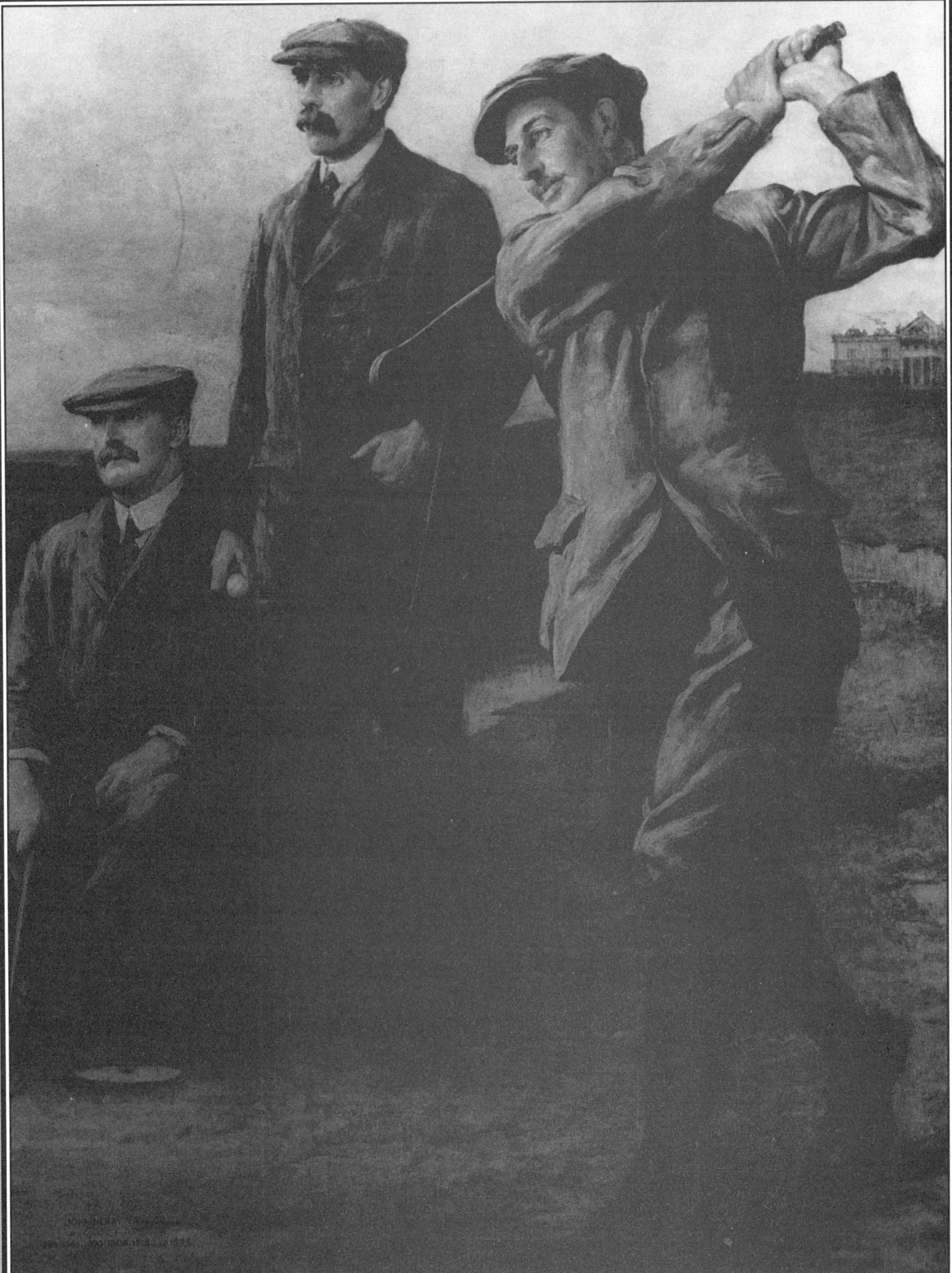

Competitors at Olton Park, Birmingham, in 1910. (Standing) Jim Hepburn, Ted Ray, George Duncan, Fred Robson, E. Veness, Arnaud Massy, J. Oke, Harry Vardon, Charles Mayo, Charlie Wingate; (seated) Rowland Jones, A. Matthews, James Braid, Tom Ball, Alex Herd, James Sherlock.

plus handicaps, while all others would play off scratch. However, the addition of another £40 of prize money for the *News of the World* Tournament in June 1904 was felt to be enough to cover the expenses of the players who qualified for the final. In a convoluted piece of logic, it was then felt that this extra prize money "obviated" the "necessity for handicaps . . . as far as that competition is concerned". If prize money was similarly increased in other tournaments "the handicapping problem would probably not be heard of again". As has been shown, this is basically what happened, and the handicapping suggestion was not heard again.

NOTES
1. *Golf Illustrated*, January 23rd, 1903
2. *Golf Illustrated*, September 4th, 1903
3. *Golf Illustrated*, August 31st, 1906

7. The Open Championship

UNTIL 1893 THE ORGANISATION OF THE OPEN Championship was the sole responsibility of the host club, of which there were three – the Prestwick Golf Club, the Royal and Ancient Golf Club and the Honourable Company of Edinburgh Golfers. It was the latter club which had taken four radical steps to transform it in 1892. It expanded the championship to 72 holes over two days instead of 36 holes in a single day; imposed an entrance charge for all competitors; moved the championship to a new green at Muirfield and increased the total prize fund from £28.50 to an advertised £100. The first three actions were taken unilaterally by the club, and the increased purse to counter a rival tournament held at Musselburgh.

In April 1893, J. McBain mused whether the Prestwick club would continue these changes instigated by the Honourable Company. He advocated that the long-term solution was to spread the burden of the cost of staging the championship by involving more clubs "to subscribe to the expenses of the Championship in return for which they would have a voice in the arrangements". He also felt that at least one of these clubs should be an English one.[1]

In the event, this is what transpired. Representatives of the three Scottish clubs met in Edinburgh on June 9th, 1893, for the purpose of "placing the competition for the Open Golf Championship on a basis more commensurate with its importance than had hitherto existed". To this end, they agreed three resolutions.

The first resolution was that two English clubs were to be invited to host the Open, St George's, Sandwich, starting in 1894, and Royal Liverpool, Hoylake, starting in 1897. The Championship would rotate between the five clubs, and would consist of four rounds of 18 holes played over two days.

The second was that each of the five clubs would contribute £15 annually towards the cost of staging the Championship, and the balance of expenses would come from an entry fee for all competitors. The prize money would total £100, with £30 for the winner, plus £10 for the cost of the gold medal, £20 for the runner-up, £10 third place, £7 fourth place, £5 fifth, £4 sixth, £3 seventh, eighth and ninth, £2 tenth and

Douglas Rolland and J.H. Taylor at the 1894 Open.

eleventh places and £1 for twelfth place.

The third resolution was that the date of each year's championship would be decided by the host club, which would also have to bear any additional necessary expenses.

The representatives of the five clubs became known as the Delegates of the Associated Clubs, and were responsible for running the Championship until the outbreak of World War I.

Thus the 1894 Open was the first one played in England, and took place at Sandwich on June 11th and 12th. There were 94 entries, of whom 90 teed off. John Ball set an early pace, with an 84 in the first round, and this was tied by J.H. Taylor and Alfred Toogood. However, playing last, Sandy Herd shot an 83 to take the lead. Rolland, whose long driving greatly entertained the crowd, and Andrew Kirkaldy both tied the course record, with 79 each in the second round. Taylor missed a short putt at the 18th to finish on 80, still good enough to leave him a shot ahead of Rolland and Andrew Kirkaldy. The latter finished in 83 in the third round, despite his approach to the last hole landing in the press tent, while weak putting condemned Rolland to an 84. Meanwhile Taylor, playing steady if not spectacular golf, finished in 81, giving him a three stroke lead from Andrew Kirkaldy and four from Rolland.

Kirkaldy started the final round in blazing style, and reached the turn in 36. However his hopes were drowned in the water hazard at the 14th hole, which cost him seven strokes. He finished with an 84, for a total of 332. Rolland improved on his morning performance, and, with a score of 82, finished on 331. At this point Taylor was on his way out, and it was reckoned he needed an 85 to be champion. Despite a seven at the 13th, when he overran the hole and hit the fence, he finished with an 81, for a total of 326. His play was characterised by straight driving and deadly approach shots.

There were 73 entrants for the 1895 Open at St Andrews, on June 12th and 13th, and again there were 12 prizes totalling £100, with the winner receiving £40, of which £10 had to be spent on the medal. As was the common practice, there were special discounted rail fares for competitors, with a return ticket being issued at "single fare and a quarter for the double journey". This applied to first-class fares for the amateurs and third-class for the professionals.

Harry Vardon was the early leader, with a first round 80, one stroke better than Andrew Kirkaldy and David Brown. Herd was two back with an 82, and Taylor finished the round on 86. Herd stormed into the lead with a 77 in the second round, despite a seven at the 5th hole due to poor putting. Taylor recovered well from his indifferent first round, with straight driving, superb iron shots and good putting, to finish with a 78. This left him tied with Kirkaldy, five strokes behind Herd. Herd was out in 39 in the third round. However at the 11th he took a six, as a result of an encounter with Strath's bunker, where he played a bold pitch that failed to clear. Nevertheless at the end of three rounds he was still three shots ahead of Taylor, who had played a steady round in 80 strokes.

Sandy Herd *c.* **1926.**

The final round came down to a straight contest between Herd and Taylor. The former added two shots to his lead in the first four holes, and then the fates intervened. The weather turned, with a strong wind starting to blow, followed by a downpour, which softened the greens. Herd had been putting beautifully on the hard greens, but was not able to find his touch when they slowed down, and finished on 85. Meanwhile Taylor found the changed conditions to his liking. His mashie approach shots constantly pitched right up to the hole, and his putting became deadly accurate. He was out in 39, and needed to come home in 42 to win. He played the 10th and 11th in three each, and the 12th in four. Sixes at the 13th and 14th slowed his progress, but then he finished in faultless manner, completing the last four holes in 17 strokes, to finish four ahead of Herd and so win his second consecutive title.

The 1896 Open was held at Muirfield, with the same prize arrangements as the previous year. The championship was played on Wednesday June 10th and Thursday June 11th. The professionals were upset when they found that they were not allowed to practise on the course on the Saturday before the championship.

Sandy Herd started in brilliant form, with a first round 72 giving him a five stroke lead over Taylor and James Kay. However in the afternoon Herd began to overhit his approach shots, his putting touch deserted him, and he finished on 84. Taylor, meanwhile, continued to play his normal precision golf, and a 78 gave him a one shot lead over Herd. Harry Vardon was six strokes behind on 161.

Taylor began the second day poorly. He pulled his tee shot into the wood on the 1st hole, and putted poorly throughout the front nine, but rallied on the back nine to finish on 81. Herd recovered his form and went round in 79, while Vardon shot his second consecutive 78. At the end of 54 holes, Herd was once again in the lead by one shot over Taylor, while Vardon was tied for fifth place, four shots behind. In the final round, Taylor, who was first out among the leaders, was once again steady, if not spectacular, and finished with an 80, for a total of 316. Once again Herd's putting touch took an afternoon nap, and was out in 42 and needed to come home in 38 to beat Taylor. But, instead of rallying, he went from bad to worse and finished on 85.

Meanwhile the unwatched Vardon was making up ground quickly. Playing with Hilton, he was out in 38, and, by the 14th hole, knew that he needed a 77 to tie with Taylor. He came to the last hole needing a five to tie, played safely, and also finished on 316. Both players were committed to play in a tournament at North Berwick on the Friday, so the play-off had to be postponed to the Saturday. It was a 36-hole competition at North Berwick, and Taylor finished tied for first place with Sayers and Willie Fernie. Vardon had a poor second round, and finished tied for ninth. Meanwhile he took the opportunity to visit Ben Sayers' shop, where he bought a new cleek with which to putt. The play-off for the Open Championship was duly held on the Saturday, and was over 36 holes. Vardon jumped out to an early lead, and, although Taylor rallied, the Jersey golfer kept his nerve to win by three strokes.

The 1897 Open was played at Hoylake on May 19th and 20th, and attracted 86 entrants. Taylor never found his form in the first round, and finished on 82; Vardon putted poorly on the fast greens, to end up on 84. Hilton and Braid both played steady golf to finish on 80, while Herd and John Ball finished on 79 to lead the field. In the second round, Braid played brilliant golf to finish on 74, while Hilton went round in 75. At the end of 36 holes, Braid was on 154, with Hilton one back and Tait four back. Taylor was eight shots behind and Vardon ten.

Vardon (white boots, back to camera) and Taylor (touching cap) on the Shelter Hole, Muirfield, play-off for the Open Championship, 1896.

In the third round, both Braid and Hilton played indifferent golf, and finished in 82 and 84 strokes respectively. Hilton went out in 38 in the final round. Coming home in 37, he finished on 314. This left Herd and George Pulford needing a 75, and Braid a 78, to win. Herd and Pulford put themselves out of contention on the front nine, taking 40 and 41 strokes. Braid was also out in 40, and needed to come home in 38, which was not out of the question. With three holes left, Braid was level and needed to play them in 14 or under. However, his third shot at the 16th overshot the green, leaving him with a nasty lie, and he took six to get down. After a five at the 17th, he needed to do the 18th in three. Braid hit his second shot with an iron right on line towards the flag. It came within a foot of the hole and then rolled passed it, stopping some six to eight yards away. Braid missed the putt and Hilton was the champion.

Again money prizes were given to the leading 12 professionals. On the day before the Open, the delegates of the five clubs "who have charge of this competition" met and recommended two important changes to the Open. The first was to shorten the prize list to six places. The winner would receive £40, of which £10 had to be spent on the medal, runner-up £20, third place £15, fourth place £10, and fifth and sixth places £7.50 each. The other change was to introduce a cut after 36 holes. The wording of the proposal was "that any competitor who is 20 strokes behind the leading score at the end of the second round on the first day of the Open Championship be compulsorily retired; but should there not be 32 professionals within this limit, then the first 32 may compete." The editor of *Golf* heartily agreed with these proposals, stating in the May 28th issue that "only ten players saw fit to retire after the first day, whereas four times that number might have stood aside without the possibility of the Champion being among them".

These changes came into effect for the 1898 Open, which was played at Prestwick on June 8th and 9th. 78 players entered the tournament. Willie Park played exceptional golf on the first day, with rounds of 76 and 75, to lead Vardon by three strokes and Taylor by five. Vardon started first on the second day, made an excellent ten-yard putt from close to the dyke at the 3rd, and went out in 36. The 15th hole cost him seven strokes when he was bunkered, and then his approach shot was short. He still finished strongly on 77. Meanwhile Park was having problems, taking six at the 1st hole, when he bunkered his approach shot, and another six at the 10th hole. However, he also finished strongly, on 78, which gave him a two shot lead over Vardon going into the last round.

In the last round, Vardon was out in 38 and back in 38, with an outstanding three for the final hole. From an awkward lie, he carried the bluff and the bunker, and then sank an eight-foot putt. He finished on 307. Park, meanwhile, had a wayward time on the 1st and 3rd holes, taking six for each. At the turn, he still led Vardon by one, but then dropped behind when he was bunkered off his drive at the 10th. He remained one behind, coming to the last hole, where he needed a three to tie. Park reached the green off the tee, and then hit a long putt three feet short of the hole. Vardon stood among the spectators as Park, who had the reputation of being one of the finest putters in game, lined up his shot. Vardon could not see through the crowd, but he knew from their reaction that Park had missed the putt. Vardon was the champion.

The rule for regulating the cut was amended on the eve of the Championship, to take effect in 1899. It now read that if there was a tie for the last place, all such ties were allowed to continue.

Many of the professionals were not happy with the revised prize money list that was produced in 1898. In August, two months after the championship, the editor of *Golf Illustrated* received a copy of a letter sent to all professionals by "a very strong Professional Committee, with Old Tom Morris at its head"[2]. This asked the Associated Clubs to consider increasing the prize money to £200, with the winner receiving £80, runner-up £40, 3rd place £25, 4th place £15, and 5th to 12th places £5 each. It suggested that if the five clubs did not "feel disposed" to adopt these proposals, they should ask other clubs to join in and share the additional "burdens entailed".

This issue appeared again on the eve of the 1899 event at Sandwich, when an announcement appeared in the press that, unless this demand for increased prize money was met, the players would strike and the championship "would be a fiasco". A meeting of the players was held, at which the motion was presented, but Vardon, Park and "the best among the professionals" were against the idea, and the ultimatum was not sent to the Associated Clubs. However, on the day before the championship, the delegates met and proposed to increase the prize money to £115, excluding the cost of the medal, the following year. (The advertised total of £125

Willie Park Junior after winning his first Open in 1887.

included the cost of the medal.) This was in recognition of some of the points raised by the professionals. An editorial in *Golf Illustrated* pointed out that "Had any such threat [to strike] been addressed to the delegates they had unanimously agreed to stiffen their backs and refuse point blank to make any increase whatever, letting the malcontents strike if they chose."[3] The modest increase in prize money was well short of what had been mooted by the players, but at least it was something.

The championship, on June 7th and 8th, went ahead with 98 entrants. Vardon, James Kinnell and Tom Williamson set the early pace, with rounds of 76 strokes. Vardon's score was attributed to long and straight driving, and to approaches of such accuracy that he left himself little to do on the greens. In the second round, he went out in 33, but could not sustain his momentum on the back nine. He started to overhit approach shots, and missed putts on the 11th, 12th and 13th holes, taking 43 strokes, to get home for a total of 76. This was still good enough to give him a one stroke lead over Taylor, and four strokes over Braid and Park.

On the second day a strong wind raised the scores in the morning, with Vardon taking 81, Taylor 83, and Braid and Park 85 each. At the end of the round, Vardon had a three shot lead over Taylor, with Kinnell, Williamson and White seven back. After an apparently much-needed lunch, Vardon found a deadly putting touch to go with the rest of his on-form game and was out in 34. As on the previous day, however, he could not sustain the momentum, and took sixes on the 12th and 15th holes, to finish with 77 for a total of 310. Jack White, with a 75 for the final round, finished second with 315.

The new prize money list was officially approved on the eve of the 1900 Open at St Andrews, which was played on June 6th and 7th. Taylor and Vardon led after the first round, with 79. Taylor improved his score in the afternoon with a 77, while Vardon went round in 81. After 36 holes, Taylor had a four stroke advantage over Vardon. Taylor increased his lead after 54 holes to six strokes, when he shot a 78, while Vardon could only manage 80. In the final round, Taylor found extra distance in his drives, to go with his precise iron shots and sure putting, and finished in 75 strokes, for a total of 309. This left Vardon too much ground to make up, and he finished second, on 317.

A record 101 players entered the 1901 Open at Muirfield, played on June 5th and 6th. Vardon set the first round pace with a 77. Taylor went round in 79, despite topping his opening drive and taking six at the 2nd. Braid went out of bounds with his first shot of the day, but came home in 36, to finish on 79. Braid made a sluggish start to the second round, but then reached the green in two at the 5th, and sank his putt for a three. This spurred him towards a 76. Vardon went round in 78, while Taylor had a poor 83. Braid and Vardon were now tied, while Taylor lay in third place, seven shots off pace. Braid found a faultless putting touch in the third round, which helped compensate for some overhitting, and he finished with a 74. Vardon began slicing his drives, and had a costly six at the 7th hole, when he fell foul of the rough, and he took 79. Taylor regained his form, and also was round in 74. Braid now held a five stroke advantage over Vardon, and seven over Taylor. The Scotsman was content to defend his lead, and went around in a safe 80, for a total of 309. Vardon could only make up two strokes, and ended the championship on 312. Much to the delight of the crowd, Braid became the first Scottish champion since Willie Auchterlonie in 1893.

The 1902 Open was held at Hoylake on June 4th and 5th, with 112 entrants. At the Delegates Meeting, the day before the tournament, it was unanimously agreed to buy a stand and case for the championship cup. The following week, a writer in *Golf Illustrated* lamented: "I must once more call attention to the mean and insignificant cup which forms the trophy for the Open Golf Championship. In design and execution it is wretched, and in every way utterly unworthy of what it represents. Will no one present a proper trophy?"[4] It is interesting how tastes change!

Despite slicing his first two shots out of bounds, Vardon set the early running with a superb 72, and at the end of the first day was four shots clear of Herd (who was using the rubber-cored ball) and Ted Ray. Braid was five back, and Taylor eight. Herd put his whole game together in the third round and shot a 73, while Vardon and Braid went round in 80, and Ray in 85. Taylor made up some ground with a 77.

Going into the final round, Herd had a three-stroke advantage over Vardon, and was eight shots clear of Taylor and Braid. As had happened too often in the past, Herd followed a good round with a poor one. Approaching and putting weakly, he went around in 81, giving him a total of 307. Meanwhile Vardon had rallied, and at the 72nd hole needed a six-

James Braid in action, Muirfield 1901.

foot putt to tie Herd. Vardon's putt reached the lip of the cup, and then stopped dead on the edge of the hole. But it was not yet over; Braid, who had started the round eight strokes behind, had been making up ground. He arrived at the last green needing a medium-length putt to tie for the championship. He too narrowly missed, and Herd was the champion.

During the championship week, an idea was mooted to change the format of the Open to include an element of match play. A report in the July 4th *Golf Illustrated* commented that "when the professionals were sounded at Hoylake as to the introduction of match play in the Open Championship they declared their preference for stroke play as at present, not so much because they objected to match play itself, but that they do not like the idea of staking their chances of winning the Championship outright or of gaining a prize on the hazards of a single round of eighteen holes . . . Were some scheme formulated to include match play, thirty six holes in the finals, with a sufficiently extended qualifying stage by strokes, I am not speaking without the book in saying that the professionals would gladly agree to it." But no more was heard of this proposal until 1904.

The 1903 Open was held at Prestwick on June 10th and 11th, and attracted 127 entrants. Once again, Vardon got off to a fast start to finish with a 73, which was equalled by Herd. In the second round, Herd had one of his characteristic poor rounds, and shot 83. Vardon continued to set the pace, and went out in 37. He dropped a shot at the 15th when he overshot the green with his approach shot, and then took seven at the 17th when he was twice bunkered and then had three putts. His 77 was good enough to give him a four shot lead at 36 holes, ahead of A.H. Scott. In the third round, Vardon reached the turn in 34. He overhit his approach shot to the 15th to drop a stroke, but came home in 38, which gave him a seven stroke lead over Jack White. In the fourth round, Vardon had his only six for the day at the 12th, when he needed two strokes to free his ball from the rough. After that, he played home safely to finish with a 78, for a total of 300. His final margin of victory was six strokes over his brother Tom. Harry Vardon's performance was all the more remarkable because he was feeling very ill during the tournament, and was barely able to finish his last round.

The idea of making the Open into a split-format tournament was raised again in *The Bystander* and *Golf Illustrated* by Ernest Lehmann and Garden Smith respectively in January 1904. They proposed that there should be a 36-hole stroke play competition, and the top 16 scores would then qualify for the match play competition. Each match would be over 36 holes. Smith, as editor of *Golf Illustrated*, solicited the opinions of the leading professionals.

Vardon was against the idea, and argued that he did not think that match play was the best test of golf because "in match play you make a very bad hole. Well, the next hole you do not play with your head as well as your club, but only with your club; the result is you find yourself, maybe, one worse still. If it had been stroke play you would have had to pay for your rashness dearly"[5]. Braid was also opposed to the idea, because he felt that there would be an element of luck in the competition, and the present conditions of the Open provided the best possible test of golf.

Herd felt that stroke play was the best test for a champion, but he did favour the concept of split-format — but with only the top eight scorers from the stroke play competition playing in the match play part. Kirkaldy came out strongly in favour of the split format, as did Ralph Smith. White was opposed to the idea, and it was J.H. Taylor who wrote the most eloquent defence of stroke play. He argued that in match play one had only to beat one's opponent, while in stroke play one had to play the entire field ". . . he is playing against an unknown quantity, and therefore it behooves him to weigh every stroke in the balances. He is playing every stroke with his brain and his whole being is at its highest tension and cannot afford to relax his efforts for one instant until the last putt is safely holed out." He felt that the 72-hole Open was "absolutely the very fairest and calls for the greatest possible skill of any scheme that can be devised".

Hilton, writing in *The Sporting Chronicle*, agreed with Taylor and company. He thought that match play might be more exciting for the spectators, but stroke play was a truer test of golfing ability. The debate carried on until March, with Horace Hutchinson pointing out in *Country Life* that those who wished to change the Open Championship were players who had not yet won it. In the end, it all remained a lively, but theoretical, debate in the pages of the press.

A special meeting of the delegates of the Associated Clubs was held on June 4th, 1904, four days before the start of the Open at Sandwich. The committee of Royal St George's felt that, with the large number of entrants (between 140 and 150), it would be impossible to complete two rounds a day. They proposed that there should be one round on the Wednesday, June 8th, and one round on the Thursday, and then two rounds on the Friday. This was agreed. The delegates met again on June 7th and recommended a change in the cut for the 1905 Open. Instead of coming at 20 strokes behind the leading score after 36 holes, the cut was to be 15 strokes behind, with the same stipulation as before – that 32 professionals were to play on the last day.

In the end there were 144 entrants, and the championship, played on June 8th, 9th and 10th, was one of the most dramatic up to this time. Harry Vardon, recovered from his illness, had a 76 in the first round, and followed this with a 73, to lead the field by two strokes. It was felt that Vardon was as long as ever off the tee, but his short game was lacking a sure touch. Robert Thomson was second, and down the list were Jack White and J.H. Taylor, six shots back, with Braid eight behind.

On the final day, Vardon's short game continued to give him problems, and he went round in 79. Meanwhile Braid caused a sensation when he played the front nine in 31. On the back nine, he dropped but a single shot, at the 16th, finishing with a record 69. White went round in 72, and Taylor in 74. As a result, Braid was the leader at the end of the round, on 226, with White on 227, Vardon on 228, and Taylor and Tom Vardon on 229. With the aid of several long putts, White did the final round in 69, to finish on 296 – the first time 300 had been broken in a 72-hole Open.

The drama was not yet over. Braid had taken 67 strokes for 17 holes for a total of 293 – three behind White. There were no scoreboards on the course, and Braid had been told, incorrectly, that White had finished on 297. On the last hole, Braid was on the green in two, and, thinking that he had a stroke in hand, played his 12-yard putt short to finish on 297. He was rather disappointed then to discover that he was a stroke behind White. Taylor was still on the course, needing an apparently impossible 67 to tie White. Playing unbelievable golf, he was on 64 after 17 holes. His putt on the 18th to tie touched the lip of the hole and rolled past. White was the champion.

The 1905 Open was played at St Andrews, over three days, on June 7th, 8th and 9th. There were 152 entrants, and the new cut rule came into effect. With a strong north-east wind blowing on the first day, no player returned a score under 80. Taylor had the best chance of breaking this until he pitched past the 17th green and into the road, ending up with a seven, which was compounded by missing a short putt at the 18th for a five. Herd and Vardon also finished on 80, along with Walter Toogood. There was a surprise leader at the end of the second day, when Rowland Jones followed his 81 with a 78 to finish one stroke ahead of Braid. Another new name, Arnaud Massy, was in third place, along with James Kinnell, two shots back. However in the third round a 78 by Braid was good enough to secure him a six stroke lead over Taylor, Massy and Kinnell. Jones, Herd and Sherlock were a further two strokes back. Braid was not really challenged in the final round. Having gone out in 38, he found bunkers at the 15th and 16th holes, and took a six at both. But a five and a four saw him home in 81, for a total of 318. Jones with a 78, and Taylor with an 80, could get no closer than five strokes, and Braid was once again the champion.

The 1906 Open was played at Muirfield, on June 13th, 14th and 15th, and there were 183 entries. Two amateurs, John Graham and Robert Maxwell, led the field after the first round, with 71 and 73 respectively. In the second round, Taylor went out in 41, but then played the back nine in 31, aided by deadly long-putting and immaculate iron shots with his mashie. After 36 holes, he had a one stroke lead over Vardon and Graham, two strokes over Duncan and Maxwell, three strokes over Jones and four over Braid. 18 holes later, Taylor was one ahead of Jones and three ahead of Vardon and Braid. Jones went out 42 and finished with an 83. Taylor started his last round poorly, when he pulled his tee shot and landed deep in a bunker. He went on to take 41 on the front nine. On the homeward nine, Taylor overran the green with his approach shot at the 11th, and then took three putts. He dropped shots at the next three holes, but then rallied. Taylor finished with a daring brassie shot at the 18th for his second, which landed next to the hole, and he was down in three. His total was 304. Vardon needed a 77 to tie Taylor for the lead. Some wayward drives and poor putting left Vardon with a 78. Braid also needed a 77 to tie, but did better than that. He was out in 38, and, helped by a long putt at the 17th for a three, came home in 35, for a winning total of 300.

The new record entry of 183 players was causing great concern among the Associated Clubs. The delegates met on the eve of the 1906 championship. W.A.R. Paterson, from Muirfield, was in the chair. He suggested that the leading professionals were as concerned as the delegates over the size of the field, and they were anxious that this should be reduced to allow the competition to be completed over two days. A scheme for holding sectional qualifying competitions was considered, "but several very considerable difficulties presented themselves as to *where*, *when*, and *by whom* these preliminary contests should be conducted". It was also pointed out that players might object to qualifying on "courses other than those on which the Championship was played". The discussion then changed tack, and the meeting favoured the suggestion that "the clubs employing professionals should be asked to discourage entries from players who had no reasonable chance of taking a prominent place in the tournament".

Then, in what was in many ways a critical turning point in the history of professional golf, the delegates agreed to seek the views of the PGA on this matter, and declared that "any suggestions it should make in furtherance of a plan for the reduction of entries should be considered by the managing clubs before any definite action was taken." Charles Mieville, secretary of the PGA, was then invited into the meeting and briefed accordingly. In 1892 and 1899 the professionals had succeeded in obtaining a larger purse in a contentious way. For the first time, through the PGA, they were now being asked for their own input about a fundamental issue concerning how the Open was run.

Arnaud Massy.

The delegates held another meeting on December 15th, 1906, and, in conjunction with a letter received from the PGA, the following decision was taken. On the Tuesday and Wednesday of the 1907 championship two qualifying rounds (or eliminating rounds, as they were called) were to be played on each day. One half of the entrants were to play on the Tuesday, and the other half on the Wednesday. The players with the 30 lowest scores from each of the qualifying groups, along with all those who tied with the 30th score, would then play in the championship, which was to be conducted over two days, on the Thursday and Friday. If a play-off was needed, it would take place on the Saturday over 36 holes. The delegates "favourably considered" the suggestion by the PGA that another links course in England be added to those over which the Open was played. However the matter was delayed, "to enable the Delegates to hear the opinion of the Committee of the Professional Golfers Association and to obtain information as to accommodation etc. at various seaside Links". And so the concept of qualifying was born.

Saxon Browne felt that this was only a partial solution to the problem. Because of the growth of professional golf, and the rapidly increasing standard of play, some method of controlling the actual number of entrants was still required.[6] This view was echoed in *The Birmingham Post*, *The Glasgow Herald* and the *Globe*. A.C.M. Croome, writing in *The Evening Standard*, expressed concern that no arrangements had been made to seed the draw for the qualifying rounds, and one venue might prove much tougher than the other. This issue was also raised in *The Manchester Guardian*.

The 1907 Open took place at Hoylake, and the number of entrants increased to 193. The qualifying rounds were played on June 18th and 19th, and the Championship itself on the 20th and 21st. The new eliminating system claimed some important scalps. Jack White failed to qualify, along with Ralph Smith, James Sherlock, George Coburn and Tom Watt, all of whom had just played in the International Match. Allowing for ties, a total of 67 players qualified for the championship.

Arnaud Massy and Walter Toogood were the first round leaders, with 76 each in terrible weather. At the end of 36 holes, Massy held a one stroke lead over Taylor and Tom Ball; Tom Williamson and George Pulford were two behind. Harry Vardon was down the field, eight behind, and Braid was ten strokes off the lead. In the third round, Taylor shot a 76, while Massy went round in 78; the Englishman now led by one shot. In the final round, Taylor sliced his second shot at the 3rd hole into the long grass and he ended up with a seven, which cost him dearly. He reached the turn in 41, and came home in 39 for a total of 314. Massy took the lead by doing the front nine in 38, and then, like Taylor, came home in 39, for a total of 312. So Massy became the first overseas player to win the Open.

The delegates met again immediately after the Open, on June 17th and then June 20th, to review the new format. Again, in consultation with the PGA, they recommended a change to the way the qualifying rounds should be played. One half of the players should play their rounds on the morning of the first day and the afternoon of the second day; the other half should play in the afternoon of the first day and the morning of the second day. Acting upon the recommendation of the PGA, the delegates agreed to write to the committees at Westward Ho! and Deal to see if they were prepared to consider holding the Open on their courses.

The delegates met again on November 16th, and recommended a further modification to the structure of the qualifying rounds. It was now felt that it was unlikely that all the rounds could be fitted into two days. They therefore proposed that the entrants be divided into three groups, and that one-third play on the Monday morning and Tuesday afternoon, one-third on Monday afternoon and Wednesday morning, and the final third on Tuesday morning and Wednesday afternoon. The top 20 players from each section would qualify. However this was not approved, and the format decided at the June 20th meeting was used. After receiving replies from both the Royal North Devon club and the Cinque Ports club, the delegates decided on Deal as the new championship course. The Open would now be played alternately in England and Scotland, and Deal would host the 1909 Open.

The 1908 Open at Prestwick attracted 178 entrants, and the modified qualifying system of two pools playing half their rounds on alternate days was used. The qualifying rounds were played on June 16th and 17th, and the championship itself on the 18th and 19th.

The first round was a low scoring affair. Ernest Gray set a new course record of 68; while Braid finished in 70 strokes, Robson in 72 and Sayers, Herd and John Ball in 74. Vardon and Taylor were well down the list, with 79 each. In the afternoon Gray did a Sandy Herd, and went round in 79, while Braid did a Braid. Once again the Scotsman played the front nine in 33. At the 13th hole, Braid hit his second shot with a cleek into the rough and took six strokes to get down. It was the only blemish in a round of 72. At the end of 36 holes, Braid had a five stroke lead over Gray, with David Kinnell and Herd a further stroke behind.

Braid had a very shaky start to his third round. He was short with his approach shot at the 1st, and took five. At the 3rd hole, he hit a cleek shot from the tee into the rough, and then failed to carry the Cardinal Bunker, using the same club. His next shot hit the sleepers and went out of bounds, and he then repeated the process after a drop. In the end, he was down in eight. After three-putting the 4th, he began his recovery. He did the 5th in two, and the next four holes in 16, to reach the turn in 39 strokes, finished the round in 77. Vardon improved his position with a 74, but at the end of the round Braid, on 219, held a six stroke lead over Tom Ball and Ted Ray. With a crowd of several thousand watching him, Braid played a splendid final round of 72, to win his fourth championship by eight shots over Tom Ball, with a record-breaking total of 291.

There were 204 entrants for the 1909 Open at Deal, which was played under the same qualifying format as the previous year. The qualifying rounds were played on June 9th and 10th, and the championship on the 10th and 11th. Charles Johns was the surprise leader after 18 holes, with a round of 72, while Taylor and Tom Ball were two strokes behind. Braid, lacking any touch with his approach shots and putts, went round in 79. In the afternoon, Taylor was on such deadly form with his approach shots that he left himself little to do on the greens. His 73 was the lowest score of the second round. After 36 holes Taylor held a one stroke lead over Johns, while Tom Ball was two back on 149 and James Braid was tied for seventh on 154.

On the second day, Taylor was out in 38, despite missing several four-foot putts. A perfect approach shot gave him a three at the 10th, and he did the 11th in five, despite finding a bunker en route. He finished strongly with two fours, for a total of 74. Meanwhile Tom Ball dropped two more strokes behind with a round of 76, and Johns fell away with a 79. Braid shot an excellent 73, but was still six strokes behind, tied for third with Johns, while Ball occupied second place, four shots adrift. Taylor continued his steady golf in the last round, and was out in 39. His best shot of the round came at the 16th hole. He heeled his tee shot into the rough, but then boldly played a brassie on to the green and was down in four. His final total of 295 was six shots better than that of Ball and Braid, who tied for second.

One of the interesting features of the championship was the birth of a golf exhibition tent, where the leading manufacturers and retailers displayed their wares. D. & W. Auchterlonie won first prize in three categories, for their drivers, brassies and wooden putters, and the Standard Golf Company, of Sunderland, won a prize for the best aluminium clubs.

At the Delegates Meeting on June 7th, 1909, a letter from the PGA which suggested that, to cut play down by a day, the scores in the qualifying rounds could be counted as the first two rounds of the championship itself was considered. It was agreed to discuss this further at a later date. They met again on February 5th, 1910, and made a radical change to the qualifying system. It was agreed that the qualifying rounds would now count as part of the championship, and that the top 60 players would compete in the last two rounds. This was a rather confusing way of putting it. What it actually meant was that the 15-stroke rule, in effect since 1905, and the qualifying round system, in effect since 1907, were both scrapped. Instead, there was now no qualifying and the cut came at the end of 36 holes with the top 60 players, and those who tied for 60th place, playing the last day.

The field on the first two days was to be split, as it had been for the qualifying rounds of the previous year, half playing their first two rounds on the Tuesday morning and Wednesday afternoon, the other half playing on the Tuesday afternoon and Wednesday morning. If the field was too large, it would be split into thirds, and an extra day added on the Monday. The format would be that proposed in November 1907. On balance, this new system was not a very good idea, as it reintroduced the old problem of the large size of the field on the first day. The prize list was extended, for the first time since 1899, to include £5 each for the seventh and eighth placed players. This brought the total purse to £125, plus £10 for the winner's medal. As the 1910 Open was to be the Jubilee Open, a special medal to the value of £10 was to be given to the winner.

Every Open champion from 1860 to 1910.

There were 210 entrants at St Andrews, played using the new format. The first day, June 21st, was washed out, so the Championship actually took place on the 22nd, 23rd and 24th. George Duncan was the early leader with 73, and Braid was tied for sixth place with a 76. Willie Smith, the Mexican-based Scot, did the second round in 71, to take the 36-hole lead with 148. Braid, having improved his score to 73, was one behind, and Duncan was on 150. The third round belonged to Duncan, who went round in 71. He now had a three stroke lead over Braid, who had a costly six at the 17th hole. Duncan fell apart in the final round, however, with sixes at the 5th and 6th holes. He finished in 83, for a total of 304. Sandy Herd, who started the round on 227, began to make up ground when he reached the turn in 35. A six at the 14th hole, and another at the 17th, ended his challenge. Braid needed a 79 to win the championship, and, after going out in 38, finished with a 76, to win his fifth Open title.

The Golf Exhibition, promoted by The Golf Agency of Edinburgh, was held again in a tent 270 feet by 60 feet set up between the Clubhouse and the sea. There were 60 exhibitors, and D. & W. Auchterlonie won the prize for the best wooden putter again, William Cunningham won the award for best brassie, Robert Forgan & Son for best driver and R. Condie for best iron. The judges were Willie Park, Charles Gibson and Peter Fernie.

St Andrews 1910. Braid plays his tee shot at the 1st in his successful attempt to be the first man to win the Open five times.

The 1911 Open at Sandwich showed the flaws of the system adopted in November 1909, as there were 226 entrants. The players had to be split into three groups, as agreed in November 1907. The first two rounds were therefore played over the Monday, Tuesday and Wednesday, June 26th, 27th and 28th, the last two rounds on the 29th. Ernest Lehman stated what should have been obvious the year before: the abolition of the qualifying rounds produced an enormous field for the first two rounds, and the tournament still required four days to complete. He felt that "some drastic alteration will eventually have to be made in the present system, as the present conditions might lead to great unfairness in the test and have become so complicated as to resemble rather a Chinese puzzle than a tournament for the World's Championship."[7]

The delegates were only too aware of the new problem which they had created for themselves. At their meeting of June 26th, 1911, they agreed to hold a special meeting later in the year to "consider the advisability of altering the conditions under which the Open Championship is now played".

Meanwhile, once all the confusion over when the A, B and C groups were to play their first two rounds had been resolved, the championship itself was rather exciting. After 36 holes, Duncan had a four stroke lead with a total of 144. Ray, Vardon and Taylor were on 148, while Hilton and Herd were on 150. In the third round, Duncan repeated his disaster of the previous year, with an 83. Vardon was the new leader, with Herd and Taylor three behind him, and Ray, Massy, Braid and Duncan four back. Hilton trailed by five.

Vardon was the first of the top players to finish the last round, shooting a poor 80 for a leading total of 303. Harold Hilton was the first contender to mount a challenge. Playing brilliantly, Hilton made up the five stroke deficit and arrived at the 18th tee needing a four to tie Vardon. On the green in three, he had a long putt for the tie, but his ball shaved the hole on the left and failed to drop. Sandy Herd came to the last tee also needing a four to tie for the lead. He recovered well from a poor drive, and was left with a six-foot putt for his four. He hit it hard and true, but the ball rattled in the hole and then popped out again. Arnaud Massy also reached the final hole needing a four to tie. In contrast to Herd and Hilton, he almost holed out in three, and was down in four.

The play-off the following day was over 36 holes. It was evenly contested for the first 13 holes, then Vardon, who was playing with great accuracy and length, started to pull away. He led by five after 18 holes, and was still ahead by that margin when Massy conceded the match at the 35th hole.

The delegates met in London on November 14th, 1911, to review the conditions of the Open Championship. They had previously written to the PGA on November 2nd, mooting the possibility that there should be a system of regional qualifying tournaments for the Open, along the lines of the *News of the World* and *Sphere* and *Tatler* tournaments. The PGA was totally opposed to this idea, and Mieville wrote to the delegates stating that the PGA had passed a resolution to the effect that "they did not consider that any qualifying rounds should be held other than at the time, and on the course on which, the Open Championship is to be played." As a result, the delegates incorporated this into yet another change in the conditions of the Open, which revived elements of the 1907 and 1909 conditions. Following the wishes of the PGA, the qualifying rounds would be played on the championship course. The scores from these rounds would not count as part of the championship. The qualifying rounds were to be played in such number of divisions as the number of entries required, and these divisions were to be as equal as possible. The players in each division would play 36 holes on the same day. The championship itself would be over 72 holes, and contested by 60 players, drawn in equal numbers from each group. It was back to either the best 30 scores from two groups, or the best 20 scores from three groups. Those tied for the last place would also compete.

This new set of conditions seemed satisfactory, and aroused little comment. However a new controversy quickly put these matters into the shadows. Harry Fulford, the Bradford professional, wrote an attack on the management of the Open in *Golf Illustrated* in December: "There are many points in connection with the running of the Championship that do not appeal to the professional." He recognised the need to have a controlling body, but protested about "what we claim to be autocratic dealings towards us". He felt there was a total disregard for the comfort of the professional players: "any shed or hurriedly-constructed compound is thought good enough for him to disrobe in." At Sandwich, the professionals' catering tent was extortionately expensive, and at least one leading player went for his lunch, paid his fee at the door, and then found that there was no food left. He argued that all these problems could be easily solved if the PGA had representation on the Committee of Management of the Associated Clubs.[8]

Garden Smith responded in the same issue. He reminded the players that "the whole meeting is practically a free gift to them from the amateurs and that it entails a great expenditure of time, labour and expense, both on the delegates and on the club over whose course the tournament is played." He rejected the idea that the PGA should have representation on the Committee of Management, as the PGA had no standing in regard to the control of the game. It was organised primarily for the mutual benefit of its members, and the funds subscribed to it by the public were for benevolent purposes. This was the crux of the structure of society at the time. The delegates could happily ask the PGA for its thoughts, but the PGA could not demand any input. As Garden Smith put it, "There is a tendency among them [the professionals] to demand as a right what they only possess as a gift."

Nevertheless, on January 9th, 1912, Mieville wrote to the Council of Delegates asking it to "be good enough to place before them this formal application that the Association [PGA] be represented on such Council." The PGA argued that it had now been in existence for ten years; had 750 members; 90% of the entrants to the Open were professionals who were PGA members, and the PGA had considerable experience in organising tournaments and in dealing with large entries. The letter was tabled at the June 24th meeting of the delegates. The application was unanimously rejected.

There were 215 entrants for the 1912 Open at Muirfield, and, under the new arrangements, they were divided into three groups. Section A played their 36 holes on Thursday June 20th. The two notable casualties were John J. McDermott, the US Open champion, and Willie Park. Section B played on Friday June 21, and Section C on Saturday June 22nd. John Ball, Harold Hilton and Robert Maxwell all failed to qualify in the last group. In all, 62 players qualified for the Championship, which began on Monday, June 24th, and finished the next day.

Ted Ray, battling around the course "with his battered Homburg hat rammed well down on his head and his beloved pipe stuck in his mouth", led after 18 holes. After another steady round in the afternoon, Ray had a three shot lead over Vardon, with Braid four behind. In the third round, Ray reached the turn in 36, but his homeward journey was rather adventurous. He missed a short putt at the 10th, and a combination of an overcautious pitch followed by a weak putt cost him a five at the 13th. He was bunkered at the 14th, 15th and 18th holes, and made it back in 40. Vardon's hope of catching him were wrecked when he took sixes at the 7th, 8th and 9th holes, where he also found bunkers on each occasion. He was

John J. McDermott's studio portrait as US Open champion, 1911.

desperately unlucky at the 8th, when his second shot landed on the green, perhaps hit a stone, and bounced at right angles into a bunker. In the end, Vardon took a total of 81 strokes for the round. Braid could not find his putting stroke until the back nine, and finished with a 77.

At the start of the final round, Ray had a comfortable lead of five strokes over Braid, seven over Duncan and eight over Vardon and Taylor. However, he faced a crisis at the 8th. Short off the tee, he hit his second into the big bunker, where the ball came to rest near the sleepers. Instead of playing cautiously, he smashed the ball out of the sand and on to the green, pin high. He finished with a 75, for a total of 295. This left Braid needing 70, Duncan 68, and Vardon and Taylor 67 to tie. No miracles were forthcoming, though Vardon went round in 71 to finish second.

Ted Ray by Quiz, 1912.

Opposite: The Golf Exhibition at Muirfield.

The PGA took over running the Golf Exhibition at the 1912 Muirfield Open, and made a sufficient profit for them to undertake it again the next year.

The 1913 Open was played at Hoylake, and attracted a record 269 entries. So, as in the previous year, there were three qualifying groups, with 20 places coming from each. The first group played on Thursday, June 19th, and 21 qualified. The notable casualty was George Duncan, who missed the cut by four strokes. The second group played on Friday June 20th, and 21 players qualified. Taylor just managed to qualify, finishing on the highest score in the group with 156. The third group played on Saturday June 21st, and 23 players emerged. The championship itself was played on Monday June 23rd and finished the next day. Ray and Taylor took the first round lead with 73s, and Taylor continued to show championship form in the second round. For example, at the 3rd hole he pulled his tee shot into a ditch, and the ball lay well under the left bank. Although he had great difficulty adjusting his stance, he hit a superb cleek shot that landed hole-high on the green. He made the turn in 36, and a less magical home journey resulted in a total of 75 strokes. Ray's round was the reverse of Taylor's. He took 40 shots on the front nine, and then came home in 34 to give him a one shot lead over Taylor.

The gale-force wind the next day favoured Taylor, who hit his shots with a lower trajectory than Ray. Taylor's score of 77 was the lowest of the round, and only the American, J.J. McDermott, could match it. Although Ray played in better conditions than Taylor, he failed to find any of his form of the previous day and went round in 81, which meant that he now trailed Taylor by three. Taylor had a shaky start to the final round, and was out in 41. The championship was essentially clinched when Taylor played the 14th hole. He pulled his second shot, but the ball landed between two bunkers. He then holed his 50-yard pitch for a three. At the same time, he received the news that Ray had just taken eight at the 3rd hole. Taylor was home in 38, for a total of 304. Meanwhile, Ray never recovered and took 84 strokes, to finish second on 312.

Whereas the qualifying system now seemed to be working, the professionals were concerned about the number of players who qualified for the championship itself. A delegation from the PGA had approached Harold Janion, secretary of Royal Liverpool, and one of the delegates, on the eve of the Open, requesting that there be an increase in the number of players who qualified. Janion responded that it was not possible to change the conditions at such a late date. He reported this at the Delegates Meeting on June 23rd. The delegates agreed that another change was needed in the conditions of the championship. One of the concerns expressed was the length of time that the championship course was occupied to the exclusion of members. It was agreed that the number of competitors in the actual championship should not exceed 100, and that they must all go through the qualifying process. A letter from Mieville to Janion was tabled in which the PGA asked to be consulted about any changes in the conditions. The delegates agreed to do so, "in accordance with recent practice". They also

The Scottish Golf Ball Manufacturing Co.'s Stall.
Makers of the Lunar and Conqueror Balls.

Messrs. R. Lehmann & Co.'s Stall.
Makers of the Zenith Balls.

The Standard Co.'s Stall.
Makers of Aluminium Putters and Clubs.

The St. Mungo Manufacturing Co.'s Stall.
Makers of the 'Colonel' Balls.

Messrs. Miller & Taylor's Stall.
Makers of the Little Model Balls.

The North British Rubber Co.'s Stall.
Makers of The Chick Balls.

J.H. Taylor.

agreed to meet again before the end of the year, to discuss changes to the conditions.

They met again on December 4th, and unanimously agreed that all entrants must qualify, and that the qualifying rounds would be played on the same day, one week before the championship, on courses close to the championship course, and the total number of players qualifying would not exceed 100. The PGA were to be informed of these changes. The two most significant were that the number of players qualifying be increased, and that the qualifying rounds would no longer be played on the championship course itself.

A follow-up meeting was held on January 17th, 1914, and a delegation from the PGA was invited to attend. This consisted of Taylor, Braid, Herd, Jack Rowe, James Sherlock, Ralph Smith and Mieville. The players

An advertisement for James Ockenden.

> # JAS. OCKENDEN
> ## HANGER HILL GOLF CLUB
> ## EALING, = = LONDON, W. 5
> Phone—Ealing 2027
>
> French Open Champion, 1923
>
> ## ALL CLUBS HAND=MADE
> Large Stock to select from
>
> ## ONLY THE BEST MATERIAL USED
>
> ## Tuition a Speciality

requested that the qualifying rounds should be played on the championship course and one other course, and that everyone would play a round on each course. They were told that this was not possible, and that the championship course would not be used for qualifying rounds.

This is precisely what happened. The qualifying rounds were held on Thursday June 11th and Friday June 12th, over Troon Old Course and

Troon Municipal Course, with the top 100 scores qualifying. Charles Mayo and Tom Renouf were the most notable players who failed to qualify. The championship itself took place at Prestwick, on June 18th and June 19th.

Vardon was the first round leader with 73, and after 36 holes he still had a stroke lead over James Ockenden, and two strokes over Taylor. Vardon and Taylor were paired together for the last day. In the third round, Taylor reversed the position, when he shot a 74 to Vardon's 78, so that now Taylor led by two.

At the start of the final round Taylor, who was distracted by the large crowd, still managed to extend his lead to three. But then, at the third hole, his concentration was broken by a photographer and he dropped a stroke. Now, once again leading by two shots, Taylor fell apart at the 4th hole. He drove into a bunker by the burn, and, although his next came out, it was resting on the edge of the burn. Taylor then found the water with his next shot, and took a seven to Vardon's four. Worse, his spirit was broken, and he dropped strokes at the 8th, 9th, 10th and 11th holes, to give Vardon a five stroke lead. Although Taylor's play recovered to some extent, Vardon won by a final margin of three strokes, to become the first, and so far the only, player to win the Open six times.

At the Delegates Meeting on June 17th, they discussed a letter that had been received from Arthur Ryle, chairman of the PGA, to discuss the 1915 Open conditions. Ryle, after conversations with Taylor, Braid, Vardon, Herd and Sherlock, suggested that the qualifying rounds be played on the Thursday and Friday of one week; practice on the championship course would take place on the Saturday and Monday; and that the actual championship be played on the Tuesday and Wednesday; that 100 players qualify for the championship; that there was a cut after 36 holes of any players more than 18 strokes behind the leader, and that the PGA were not opposed to a rise in the entrance fee. The delegates agreed with the proposed timetable, but not with the other points. They proposed that only 80 players should qualify, which would make a cut unnecessary. They were not proposing to increase the entry fee. The debate over the Open conditions abruptly ceased with the outbreak of war.

NOTES
1. *Golf*, April 28, 1893
2. *Golf Illustrated*, August 12th, 1898
3. *Golf Illustrated*, June 16th, 1899
4. *Golf Illustrated*, June 13th, 1902
5. *Golf Illustrated*, February 12, 1904
6. *Golf Illustrated*, December 21st, 1906
7. *Golf Illustrated*, July 7th, 1911
8. *Golf Illustrated*, December 8th, 1911

8. Major PGA Tournaments

The *News of the World* Tournament

AT THE BEGINNING OF AUGUST 1903, THE PGA Committee announced that "the well known newspaper, the *News of the World* . . . [has] generously offered, with a view to encourage match play among professional golfers, the sum of £200 to be competed for at a match play tournament, limited to members of the Association." It was to be held at Sunningdale on October 13th to October 15th, 1903. And so was born the *News of the World* Tournament, which immediately became the second most important event of the year, next to the Open.

The format was simple. The final would consist of 32 players, and was match play. The first four rounds were over 18 holes, and the final was 36 holes. The whole final event lasted three days, and in this period was always played on a major course near London. The 32 players had to qualify in sectional stroke play tournaments. Each of the PGA sections was allotted a set number of places. In 1903 there were five sections: Irish, Scottish, Northern, Midland and Southern. The Welsh section was added in 1905, the Western section in 1909 and the Eastern section in 1910. As the number in the final was fixed at 32, constant adjustments were made to the number of players qualifying from each section, on a proportional basis that reflected the membership in each region.[1]

The total prize in 1903 was £200, with the winner receiving £100, the runner-up £30, the semifinalists £15 each and the quarter-finalists £10 each. The purse was increased the following year to £240, so that the second round losers could receive £5 each. Those knocked out in the first round did not receive anything until 1911, when the purse was increased to £400. The winner still received £100, but the runner-up now won £40, the semifinalists £20 each, the quarter-finalists £15 each, the second round losers £10 each and the first round losers £5 each.

The qualifying tournaments became very important regular events in their own right. Thus the *News of the World* Tournament actually added six, and ultimately nine, tournaments a year to the annual schedule. It also created a format that was repeated for the *Sphere* and *Tatler* Cups, and the Perrier Assistants Tournament. The qualifying tournaments varied in the size of the fields. The smaller sections – Scotland, Ireland, Wales, Eastern

England and Western England – had relatively small entries, usually between 20 and 40. The Midlands section usually had around 60 to 70 entries; the Northern around 30 in the early years, but up to 84 in the later years; and the Southern field grew from 78 in 1903 to a peak of 155 in 1911. The Southern section field had grown so large by 1910 that it had to be split into two groups on different courses, with each half competing for six places. There was a total of 164 entrants in all the tournaments in 1903, and the number had grown to 390 in 1910. As mentioned earlier, the qualifying tournaments often included a regional championship.

In 1907 the great popularity of the final tournament with both the public and the players was attributed to "the interesting and searching nature of the test of golf".[2] The significance of winning the finals was great. Harry Vardon described winning the 1912 tournament as having realised "one of the ambitions of my golfing life".[3]

1903 Tournament

The 1903 tournament was played at Sunningdale, on October 13th, 14th and 15th. Vardon was absent due to illness, and the major casualties in the qualifying tournaments were Andrew Kirkaldy, Ben Sayers and James Kinnell. The surprise victim in the first round was Jack White, playing on his own course, who was beaten by Tom Williamson. Taylor, Braid, George Coburn and Ted Ray all reached the semifinals. Braid was drawn against Taylor, who, suffering from stiffness due to the soaking he had got in the morning rain, lacked both distance and accuracy in his driving. Braid beat him 4 and 2. Meanwhile Ray disposed of Coburn by 4 and 3.

In the final, Braid and Ray were even after nine holes, and the Scotsman held a one hole advantage after the first round. At the 1st hole of the second round, Ray missed his approach shot to the green, and that cost him the hole. At the 3rd, Braid sent his drive into the rough, but reached the green with his second shot and made his long putt to go three up. Braid still held that lead after nine holes. The 10th saw the beginning of the end. Ray hit his drive straight down the middle of the course. Braid drove his into a bunker about 200 yards from the green, and then hit a superb iron shot to within two yards of the hole. He was down in three, while Ray took two putts for a four. Ray managed to win the 12th, but lost the 13th, and Braid went on to win 4 and 3.

1904 Tournament

In 1904 the tournament came to Mid-Surrey, on October 4th, 5th and 6th. Kirkaldy, Tom Vardon and Jack White, the ailing Open Champion, all failed to qualify for the finals. Sayers and Massy were drawn together in the first round, and the two men saw no point in both travelling south from North Berwick. They tossed a coin to see who should make the trip, and Sayers won the call. There were no major upsets in the first round, but Braid was drawn against Herd in the second round, and the defending champion was beaten by one hole. The match was decided at the 10th, when Braid pulled his tee shot and landed in the rough. He took two to get out, and Herd had a one hole lead, which was good enough to decide the outcome. In the quarter-finals, Herd defeated Vardon at the 19th hole, when the latter missed a three-yard putt, while Ray was beaten by Alfred Toogood.

In the semifinals, Toogood beat Hepburn by 4 and 2. Taylor defeated Herd on the last hole of their match by sinking a seven-foot putt after Herd played a superb bunker shot to lay his ball stone dead. On the day of the finals there was a strong wind, which favoured Taylor, who was considered the master of the low trajectory drive. Toogood, on the other hand, was plagued by wild driving, and was seven holes down after 18. He made a fight of it in the afternoon, but Taylor won easily by a margin of 5 and 3.

1905 Tournament
The 1905 final was held at Walton Heath, starting on October 3rd. Jack White once again lost in the first round, but the big match in that round was Braid against Herd. They were square after 18 holes, and Braid won at the 19th, when his putt for a three dropped in, after apparently coming to stop on the lip. In the second round, Rowland Jones won the first two holes against Harry Vardon, and held on to that lead to win by a hole. Vardon was plagued by poor short-putting.

Ultimately Braid played Tom Vardon in the final. In contrast to his brother's problem, Tom Vardon's greatest asset on the day was his short game. He took the 1st hole when he reached the pin with his approach shot. He won the 3rd hole, when he pitched to the hole from the rough, while Braid three-putted. Vardon was three up after four holes, but the tide soon changed. Braid trailed by a hole at the turn. Vardon failed to come to terms with the wind on the return, and began driving wildly. Braid made up three holes to lead by one after 18. In the second round, Braid was still three up at the turn. Poor putting by Braid at the 10th and 12th reduced his lead to a single hole with six to play, but then Vardon imitated his brother. He putted poorly to give away one hole, and another expedition into the rough at the 14th gave Braid a three hole lead with four to play. Braid won the 15th when he laid his approach shot dead from a difficult lie, and took the match by 4 and 3.

1906 Tournament
The 1906 final was held at Hollinwell, starting on October 2nd. In the first round, George Duncan pulled off a major upset by defeating Braid by 3 and 2, Braid playing loosely and stymied on four holes. Ted Ray also lost in the first round, going out to the unheralded A. Catlin from Mid-Herts.

In the second round, Herd defeated Harry Vardon by two holes. Duncan claimed the scalp of another member of the Triumvirate, defeating Taylor by one hole. Herd then had an easy win against Duncan in one semifinal, by 6 and 5, while Charles Mayo defeated Rowland Jones in the other by 2 and 1. The final itself was a very one-sided affair, Herd winning easily by 8 and 7.

Fred Robson at the 1926 Ryder Cup.

1907 Tournament

The 1907 final was once again held at Sunningdale, starting on October 15th. Tom Vardon, the 1905 finalist, failed to qualify, as did James Hepburn. Mayo put out Duncan in the first round by 5 and 4. Herd was beaten in the second round by the Irish champion, James Edmundson. The semifinals matched Braid against Ray, and Taylor against Harry Vardon. Ray found Braid unstoppable. He played the front nine in only 33 strokes, to lead by a hole at the turn, and, when Ray's game fell off, took the match by 4 and 3. The other semifinal came down to the last hole. Vardon put his drive into a bunker, which left him a little too much to do. Taylor won the hole and match.

In the final, the lead changed hands several times, and, after 18 holes, Braid and Taylor were all square. Braid started well after lunch, and won three out of the first four holes. The match turned on the 13th hole. Taylor was two down with six to play, and then played a lovely cleek shot, which ran a few yards past the hole, while Braid put his shot into the rough about 30 yards from the pin. Playing a perfect pitch, Braid was left with a tap-in. Taylor overhit his putt, and then needed another two strokes. Instead of being one down with five to play, he was three down, and Braid went on to win the match by 4 and 2.

1908 Tournament

The 1908 final was again played at Mid-Surrey, beginning on October 6th. In the first round Tom Vardon beat Herd at the 19th hole, after the latter was dormy 2, and Tom Ball defeated Massy by 4 and 3. However the biggest match of that round was Taylor against Braid. They were level after 14 holes. Poor iron play and poor putting by Braid gave Taylor the 15th hole, then wayward driving by the Scotsman gave Taylor the 16th as well. Taylor held on to win by 2 and 1. Fred Robson made his presence felt in the second round, when he disposed of Tom Ball. Taylor had a close match, with Ray winning by two holes. In the third round, Mayo beat Vardon, who was putting poorly yet again, by 4 and 3. In the semifinals, Taylor beat Sherlock by 3 and 2, and Robson defeated Mayo by 3 and 1. In the final, Robson played inspired golf during the first round, and took a three hole lead over Taylor. Taylor began a spirited fight back in the second round, winning the 2nd, 3rd, 4th and 5th holes, to go one up. By the turn, he was three up. Robson recaptured some of his earlier form and reduced Taylor's lead to one over the next two holes. But Robson missed a long putt at the 13th, which would have tied the match, and actually lost the hole. He won the 14th, but the next three were halved, so at the 18th Robson was still one down. He drove into the rough and then found a bunker with his next shot, leaving Taylor little to do to win both the hole and the match.

1909 Tournament

Between 1903 and 1908, the *News of the World* trophy stayed in the hands of either Braid, Taylor or Herd, who were now viewed as the old guard. This state of affairs came to an end in 1909. In the Southern section quali-

Tom Ball, second in the Open Championship, 1908.

fying tournament, Vardon had to play off with four others for the final spot, and Duncan failed to qualify. The finals were held at Walton Heath, starting on October 5th. They began in a sensational manner. Braid was easily beaten in the first round on his home course by Jack Rowe, and Taylor also exited at that stage, losing at the 20th hole to James Hepburn.

In the semi-finals, Herd was drawn against Harry Vardon, and Tom Ball against Hepburn. In his match with Herd, Vardon once again had big problems with little putts. He missed a four-foot putt, to give Herd the first lead of the day at the 7th hole. They were level again at the 11th, and then Vardon took the lead at the 12th. Herd drew level at the 16th, when Vardon sliced his drive into the rough. Vardon then missed the chance to win the 17th, when he failed to hole a three-foot putt. All square at the last hole, Vardon missed a six-foot putt to save the hole, and thus lost the match. Ball took an early lead against Hepburn, and was two up at the turn. He went three up at the 10th, when Hepburn was bunkered to the left of the green. Ball took the 11th, and the match was virtually settled when Hepburn missed a four-foot putt at the 12th. Ball won by 5 and 4.

In front of 2,500 spectators for the final, Ball and Herd matched shot for shot for ten holes. At the 11th hole, Ball laid a stymie, and took the lead for the first time. He went two up at the 13th, when he holed an 18-yard putt; and then three up, when Herd missed a short putt at the 15th. Ball quickly pulled away at the start of the second round, winning the 1st hole with the aid of a perfect pitch shot. At the 2nd hole, Herd put his brassie shot into the bracken and his third shot hit a spectator, the ball rebounding into the rough. Herd's problems continued when he lost the 3rd hole, after neatly placing his drive into a cart rut. Herd then won the next two holes, to pull within four. Then at the 6th Herd sent his first shot into the bunker at the left of the green, and, lying badly, took three to recover. Ball actually hit his tee shot over the green and on to the 17th hole teeing area, but recovered nicely and was down in two from there. Ball still led by five at the turn, and won the match by 7 and 5.

1910 Tournament
Braid failed to qualify for the 1910 finals at Sunningdale, which started on October 4th. In the first round, Ray was beaten by Herd, who in turn was beaten by James Sherlock in the second round. Tom Ball defeated Vardon at the 20th hole in the same round. In the third round, Duncan stopped Ball's run with a 3 and 1 victory. However, the biggest upset of the round was the defeat of Taylor, who was nursing an injured wrist, by young Cyril Hughes from Chester, who won by 3 and 2. Hughes took Duncan to the 19th hole in the semifinals before going down, while Sherlock won his match against Eric Bannister, who had a soft draw to reach that stage. In the final, Duncan was wildly off-line with his driving in the first round, found his rhythm at the start of the second round, but misplaced his putting touch in the process. Sherlock won easily by 8 and 6.

1911 Tournament
Taylor and Ball both failed to qualify for the 1911 finals, which were held at Walton Heath, starting on October 3rd. The finals were scheduled to be played at Mid-Surrey, but the venue was changed because of fears that some recent alterations to the course could be damaged by the crowds. Sherlock, the defending champion, beat Herd in the first round, but went out in the second round to Tom Williamson. Duncan did not play because he was on his tour of America. Nevertheless, he was given a £5 prize for having qualified. Hughes, the surprise of 1910, reached the third round, before he was beaten by Harry Vardon, and Tom Ball was beaten in the same round by Braid.

Ted Ray was matched against Harry Vardon, and James Braid against Tom Williamson, in the semifinals. In what was becoming the annual description of Vardon's play in this tournament, his inability to sink short putts was his undoing against Ray, and he lost by 3 and 1. James Braid was also having trouble putting in his match, and Tom Williamson led by two holes with three to play. However Braid rallied to win the 16th and 17th holes, so the match was even at the last hole. Williamson maintained his concentration, and was unlucky not to hole his putt for the match. Braid finally found his putting touch at the 22nd hole, sinking a 14-foot putt to win the match.

The competition in progress at Aldeburgh in 1911.

In a closely-fought final, Ray came unstuck at the third hole of the final round, when he was one down. He topped his approach shot, and the ball woke up some earthworms before coming to a stop in a bunker. Nothing went right for Ray after that, and he found himself six down with nine holes left to play. At the 10th, Ray suddenly remembered where he had left his putting touch and began his comeback, reducing the deficit to a single hole with but one left to play. Both were on the green in two, and Ray struck his six-yard putt beautifully; but it stopped three inches short of the hole. Braid placed his putt stone-dead, and, with the hole halved, Braid was the victor. Afterwards Braid commented, "This match has made me properly shake."

1912 Tournament

Braid, Tom Ball, Rowland Jones, Mayo and Sherlock all failed to qualify for the 1912 finals, which were held at Sunningdale, starting on October 2nd. Taylor crashed out in the first round, losing to Jack Rowe, and Duncan was beaten by Vardon. Vardon then defeated Herd in the third round and R.G. Wilson in the semifinal. Ray vanquished H. Cawsey in the other semifinal.

The final itself was as tense and dramatic as the previous year. Vardon was three up after the first 18 holes, then Ray reduced this to two up with nine left to play. At the 11th, Ray was wildly off-line with his drive, but benefited from a free drop, when his ball landed in casual water. He proceeded to hit a magnificent shot over the trees, and ran his putt in for a three, to reduce Vardon's lead to one. Ray played the 13th hole in two, to square the match with five to play. At the 14th, Vardon played a wonderful approach putt that enabled him to take the hole. Vardon sank another good putt at the 15th, to go two up. At the 16th, Vardon hit a weary drive, and played an equally tired approach shot into a bunker. Ray was on the green in two, but ran his approach putt a yard or so past the hole. Vardon came out of the sand and then missed the ensuing long putt. Ray's putt to win the hole refused to take the plunge, after hovering on the lip, and Vardon was able to escape with a half. At the 17th, though, Ray was able to pull within one hole, when Vardon jerked at a putt and missed it. At the final hole, though, he made the putt he needed to win the tournament. For the second year in a row Ray had lost a long and gruelling final.

Taylor, Robson and Herd all failed to qualify for the 1913 finals, which were held at Walton Heath, starting on October 7th, and neither Vardon nor Ray took part, as they were both in America. Tom Ball lost in the first round to young Ernest Whitcombe. R.G. Wilson reached the semifinal for the second year in a row, and lost again, this time to Duncan by 4 and 3. In the other semifinal, Braid defeated the young Scot, Willie Watt.

In the final, Duncan took an early lead, when he won the 2nd hole. Braid levelled the match at the 4th hole, after Duncan hit a weak recovery shot from a sliced drive, and they were still level at the turn. Braid won the 10th hole, but Duncan promptly won the 12th, 13th and 15th holes, with the aid of beautiful approach shots at the last two. At the end of the first round, Braid was two down. Duncan increased his lead to four holes at the 4th, when he stymied Braid. Braid reduced the lead to three holes, but that was as close as he could get, and Duncan won by 3 and 2.

Only the Western section Qualifying tournament was played in 1914, before the outbreak of World War I.

The *Sphere* and *Tatler* Cups

The *News of the World* Tournament was primarily a late season event, with 86% of the qualifying tournaments taking place in July or September, and the finals taking place in October. In 1911 the PGA announced a new tournament for its members to occupy the spring months of March, April and May. It would also take advantage of the already-demonstrated growing popularity of foursomes events. The new tournament was sponsored by the proprietors of the *Sphere* and *Tatler* magazines, and was to be known as the *Sphere* and *Tatler* Cups. It was to be a foursomes tournament, with a total purse of £350, and organised along similar lines to the *News of the World* Tournament. There were to be 64 finalists, who qualified via eight sectional tournaments, like the *News of the World* Tournament.[4] There the similarity stopped. Although the players qualified in stroke play tournaments as individuals, the final was between 32 teams playing two-ball foursomes match play. What was even more unusual was that the partners were decided by a random draw, literally out of a hat. The winners received £50 each, and runners-up £15.75 each. There were then four prizes of £8.40; eight of

£6.30; 16 of £4.20 and 32 of £2.20. Therefore, every player who reached the final tournament received a prize. In the press announcement launching the new tournament it was described as "a welcome variation on the somewhat monotonous string of stroke play competitions which the professionals engage in every year".

The prize money distribution remained constant for the four years of the tournament. The number of entries for the qualifying tournaments was very similar to the size of the fields for the *News of the World* tournament.

The Southern section had the largest number of entries, with a peak of 156 in 1911, and the Northern and Midlands sections each exceeded 80 entrants in 1912 and 1913. In 1912, the Southern section qualifying tournament had to be split into two groups, to cope with the number of players. As with the *News of the World*, the *Sphere* and *Tatler* Cups added nine tournaments a year to the calendar, although again some of the qualifying tournaments were also sectional championships. The Midlands qualifying tournament was also for the Challenge Cup, the Northern was for the Leeds Cup and the Southern was also for the Tooting Bec Cup.

Braid, Taylor and Vardon were all paired with virtual unknowns in the 1911 finals, held at Walton Heath on May 16th, 17th and 18th. Taylor and W. Hambleton reached the final, defeating Braid and H.A. Richards in the quarter-finals, and George Duncan and David Grant in the semifinals, at the 20th hole. In the other semifinal, James Bradbeer and Sandy Herd defeated W. Leaver and Wilfrid Reid, who had beaten Vardon and J.W. Gaudin in the second round. Herd and Bradbeer won the final handily by 8 and 7.

The 1912 final was played at Hoylake, starting on May 14th. Braid was drawn with C.T. Roberts from Woolton, Vardon with the Irish professional H. McNeil, and Taylor with R.A. Gray from Benton. Duncan and Sherlock were paired together, and were considered pre-tournament favourites, along with Herd and Davie Grant, Peter Rainford and Jack White, and J.B. Batley and F.H. Frostick. Braid and Roberts played Vardon and McNeil in the first round and beat them by a single hole. The critical shot came at the 16th hole, when Vardon fluffed his mashie shot to the green to put them two holes down. Vardon and McNeil won the 17th, but Vardon missed the decisive nine-foot putt at the last hole. Taylor and his partner were beaten by Ben Sayers and W.P. Lewis in the first round as a result of Sayers' uncanny putting.

The final saw Braid and Roberts against Duncan and Sherlock. Braid and Roberts held a one-hole advantage early on which they lost when Braid drove out of bounds at the 7th. They then went one down, when Braid topped his tee shot at the 9th. At the end of the first round, Duncan and Sherlock were three up. The match was virtually decided when Duncan and Sherlock won the first two holes of the second round to go five up, and they went on to win by 4 and 2.

Sherlock and Fred Robson failed to qualify for the 1913 final, which was played at Deal, from May 20th. The first round produced a string of upsets. Braid and P.J. Gaudin were beaten by R.G. Wilson and the rising Welsh

James Batley.

professional, George Gadd; Ray and J.W. Whiting went out to Joshua Taylor and B.F. James; Herd and J. Bloxham lost at the last hole to A.J. Lewis and A.E. Hallam. In contrast to previous years, Taylor had drawn Duncan as his partner, and Vardon was paired with the veteran Midland player, Tom Williamson. Taylor and Duncan disposed of Mayo and S. Whiting in the first round; W.T. Jefferies and S. Ball in the second; and Harry Fulford and P.E. Taylor in the third round.

In the semifinal the wind continued to blow hard, when Taylor and

Duncan came up against Vardon and Williamson. The latter pair were down by two after two holes, but won the 3rd, when, as Duncan grounded his club to address his second shot, the ball moved. The match turned at the 11th hole, when Vardon and Williamson were one down. Duncan found the bunker in front of the green with his tee shot on this short hole, while Williamson's shot went over the green and into a far bunker. Taylor pitched out of the near bunker, over the green and into the far bunker, and the match was soon level. Williamson then holed two successive long putts to put his team into the final. In the other half of the draw, Joshua Taylor and James progressed to the semifinal, where they defeated Wilson and Gadd at the 19th hole. In the final Vardon and Williamson were too strong for Taylor and James, and overwhelmed them by 7 and 5.

The 1914 finals were played at Sunningdale, from May 13th. Taylor, who was unwell, was paired with Tom Williamson, but they were routed in the first round by the very strong team of Ray and Duncan, by 8 and 6. In the second round, Braid and R.S. Fernie were beaten by Mayo and Fox, while Len Holland and J.B. Batley took advantage of Vardon's poor putting to defeat him and Joshua Taylor by 4 and 2. In the third round, Ray and Duncan took on Herd and J. Cheal, and the former pair were down by four after six holes. They then rallied, and squared the match at the 17th. Alas, Duncan played a critical short putt too casually at the 20th, and he and Ray were beaten. Herd and Cheal were unable to find the same form when they played Holland and Batley in the semifinal. The match was decided on the back nine, where Batley and Holland converted a one hole deficit into a two hole lead by the 14th hole, and went on to win by 3 and 2. This was mainly the result of poor play by Cheal, who instituted a policy of seeking bunkers from the tee, leaving Herd too much to do.

The final was between the relatively unknown teams of Batley and Holland and George Smith and C. McIntosh. The latter pair were only one down after the 6th hole of the second round; but then they began to fall apart, and Batley and Holland won by 5 and 4. Batley played a steady, accurate game, while Holland gave valuable assistance, especially with his approach putts. Both Smith and McIntosh were wild off the tee, and Smith was persistently short with his approach putts.

Harry Vardon attributed the failure of Duncan and Ray to win the 1914 finals to the fact that Ray "will put his partner into some horrible places – places that he himself with his Herculean strength and extraordinary power of recovery, would have no difficulty in getting out of, but to his partner it would be a serious proposition to tackle".[5]

The comments in *Golf Illustrated* about the 1914 finals were an apt summary of the whole concept of this tournament: "The *Sphere* and *Tatler* foursomes have shown conclusively from their very beginning that individual merit is of less importance than a judicious combination . . . To the average spectator, perhaps, the absence of the cracks in the later stages was disappointing; but the exposition of foursome play was in no wise injured by this absence, and the tournament is serving a good purpose in showing that our professionals have not mastered the whole art of golf."

The Tooting Bec Cup.

The Tooting Bec Cup

The Tooting Bec Cup, on October 15th, 1901, was the first competition held by the nascent PGA, when it was still called the London and Counties Professional Golfers Association. It was a 36-hole stroke play tournament, and the cup itself was presented by the Tooting Bec Golf Club. The first tournament was held at the Tooting Bec Club itself. Jack White, James Hepburn and Ernest Gray were the first round leaders with 75. Taylor, despite an inauspicious six at the 1st hole – followed by several missed putts at the subsequent holes – still managed to go round in 76. Braid had a mistake-filled 80, which he immediately atoned for in the second round when he recorded a 73, for a total of 153. However, this only brought out the best in Taylor, who was playing behind him, and he too had a 73 for a total of 149. Rowland Jones, who had also gone round in 80 in the morning, had the lowest score of the day, with a 72, for a total of 152, which gave him a tie for second place along with James Hepburn.

By the time the event was held the following year on September 17th, 1902, it was now a PGA Southern section tournament, and was played at Romford. Braid, playing on his home course in a strong wind, finished on 148, six strokes ahead of Ralph Smith and seven ahead of Taylor.

The 1903 tournament was held at Hanger Hill Golf Club on May 12th. Taylor had a poor morning round and tore up his card in the afternoon. It was felt that he was probably stale from playing too many exhibition matches. Braid won for the second year in succession. He and Vardon led after the first round, with scores of 73. Vardon went round in 78 for the second round, lacking the accuracy in approach shots that he had shown in the morning. Braid finished strongly with a 75, for a score of 148, three better than Vardon's.

The 1904 tournament was held at West Middlesex Golf Club, on May 4th. This tournament was unique for the period in that some of the professionals were given handicaps. The man who benefited most from this was the Hampstead professional, J. McLaren, who was playing off three. His gift of six strokes over the two rounds was enough to allow him to tie Braid on 147. An 18-hole play-off followed, apparently on the same day, and McLaren was still allowed his handicap of three. Much to everybody's surprise, the players were tied coming to the last hole, but then the pressure finally got to the young Hampstead pro. He topped his drive into the pit in front of the teeing area, and his ball disappeared forever. Going back to the tee, he took a drop and then still played short of the green. Braid drove on to the green and was down in three, clinically to clinch the tournament. The experiment of allowing handicaps was never repeated in a major tournament in this period.

The 1905 tournament was held at Northwood Golf Club, on May 3rd. Braid set the first round pace with a 74. Vardon reached the 17th tee in 62 strokes, only to make a complete mess of the last two holes, playing them in 14 instead of the expected nine, to finish with a 76. Braid took 79 strokes in the afternoon, for a total of 153, but it quickly became apparent that this

A.H. Toogood.

score was unlikely to be good enough. Taylor was out in 34, while Alfred Toogood was out in 36. Toogood, with putting that was reminding spectators of Walter Travis in the 1904 Amateur Championship, finished on 73, and was the clubhouse leader with 150. Taylor still had a very good chance of beating that total, if he could play the last five holes in 23. Bad luck with putts and a missed approach shot meant that he needed a four at the last hole to tie Toogood. He was on the green in two, but under-hit his approach putt. His next putt, to tie Toogood, kissed the lip of the cup, but went no further. Toogood was the winner.

The 1906 tournament was held at Ashford on April 25th, and, for the first time, none of the Triumvirate was in the field. The favourites in their absence were Toogood, Jones and White. Toogood, who led after the first round with 75, fell apart in the afternoon and recorded an 83, for a total of 158. The surprise winner was W.A. Lonie, a 43-year-old Scot based at Rye, and a club professional of no repute. He finished on 152, four shots clear of Wilfrid Reid. He owed his fleeting day of fame, in raw windy conditions, to keeping his not-particularly-long drives on line, and following up with steady approach shots.

The Triumvirate all competed in the 1907 tournament, on May 15th at Totteridge. Braid took the first round honours with a 74. Taylor was well down the list, nine strokes behind. In a stunning second-round reversal, he took 12 strokes off his morning score with a 71, and a total of 154. However, Braid went round in a steady 77, and held on to his lead, to finish three shots ahead of Taylor. Vardon finished fourth on 157.

The 1908 tournament took place at Neasden, on May 14th. Braid and Taylor finished fifth and sixth respectively. In an exciting finish, Rowland Jones and Ernest Gray tied for the lead on 153, one shot better than Duncan and Mayo. Jones won the play-off by a single stroke. Vardon did not enter.

The 1909 tournament was at Maidenhead on May 12th, and neither Vardon nor Duncan competed. Braid broke the course record in the morning with a 71. Then, in the afternoon, he undoubtedly felt like breaking his putter, when a poor performance with that club condemned him to an 82. Sherlock, who had been three shots behind in the morning, played a good steady round in the afternoon for a 75, which gave him a four stroke victory over Braid.

By 1909, the tournament was viewed as an important and popular event in its own right. There were 46 entries in 1901, and that figure rose quickly to 87 by 1903. There was a peak of 93 in 1908, and in 1909 there were 73 entries. The 1910 tournament was scheduled to take place at Banstead Downs on May 11th, and a record 117 players had entered. At this point an event occurred that permanently altered the tournament. King Edward VII died on May 6th, and, as a mark of respect, the tournament was postponed. Because of the crowded schedule of tournaments and exhibitions, the PGA decided that the only practical option was to hold the challenge for the cup concurrently with the Southern section *News of the World* qualifying tournament, which was to be held on July 20th at Stoke Poges. Playing on his home course, James Sherlock successfully retained the cup. His first round 75 was one behind the leaders, E.P. Gaudin and Charles Johns. Sherlock then set a new course record in the afternoon with a 73, for a total of 148. The course record only lasted an hour or so, until Tom Vardon finished his round in 71; but Sherlock's 148 was good enough to secure the victory by a margin of four strokes ahead of Mayo, Tom Ball, Tom Vardon and E.P. Gaudin. Duncan and Vardon finished eighth, Taylor 10th and Braid down the list in 17th place.

In 1911 it was decided to hold the challenge for the cup as part of the Southern section *Sphere* and *Tatler* qualifying tournament, at Banstead Downs on May 3rd. Vardon's putting was teribly erratic. In the morning round, he putted brilliantly and turned in a 72, but in the afternoon nothing went down, and he finished in 82, for a total of 154. With the weather deteriorating by the hour, Wilfrid Reid's pair of 77s was good enough to tie Vardon, and force a play-off two days later. Reid, playing on his home course, was out in 37 for a three-stroke lead, but Vardon rallied splendidly to win by two strokes.

In 1912 the Southern section *Sphere* and *Tatler* qualifying tournament was split into two sub-sections, one to play at West Herts and one at Purley Downs, both on April 24th. The winners of the two tournaments would then play-off for the Tooting Bec Cup at a later date. Braid came first at

Purley Downs, finishing on 147, four shots ahead of Ray. P.J. Gaudin won at West Herts, also finishing on 147, one stroke ahead of Duncan. Gaudin won the cup, although records of the play-off have proved to be rather elusive to the present writer.

The same format was used in 1913, with the two *Sphere* and *Tatler* qualifying tournaments taking place on May 7th, at Denham and Fulwell. Vardon and J.B. Batley tied for first at Denham, on 152 each, and Ray and Rowland Jones tied for first at Fulwell, with 145 each. The play-off for the cup was not actually held until April 14th, 1914, when the four players met at Thorpe Hall. This resulted in another tie, with Ray and Batley finishing on 74, while Jones and Vardon took 77 and 78 respectively. Ray and Batley played again on April 20th, at Old Ford Manor. Here Ray finally won the 1913 Tooting Bec Cup, almost 12 months later.

Two days later, on April 22, it was time to play for the 1914 Tooting Bec Cup. The same format as in the previous two years was used again. The two *Sphere* and *Tatler* qualifying tournaments were held at Old Ford Manor and Worplesdon. Charles Johns and R. Gray tied for the lead at Old Ford Manor, on 152, while Vardon finished first at Worplesdon. The three men were then scheduled to play-off for the 1914 Tooting Bec Cup. There is no record of this having taken place. If the scheduling was similar to 1913, war would have broken out before a date had been settled.

Perrier Water Assistants' Tournament

For those who thought that Perrier Water was an adman's bonanza of the 1970s, it might come as something of a surprise to learn that Perrier sponsored what could be viewed as the first junior professional tournament, beginning in 1910. It began life as an open letter from "The Proprietors of Perrier Water" to the editor of *Golf Illustrated,* published on March 10th, 1910, stating: "It has occurred to us that a competition entirely confined to the apprentices and assistants [of professional golfers] would help to give these young players the opportunities they now lack [to compete in tournaments], and we should be happy to present prizes to the sum of 100 guineas for this purpose." The letter requested the editor to bring this proposal to the attention of the PGA. This was done with great speed.

As to be expected, it was organised along the same lines as the existing *News of the World* and subsequent *Sphere* and *Tatler* tournaments. There would be a final, consisting of 16 players who had qualified through the PGA's geographic sections. Seven players would qualify from a Southern tournament, three from the North, two from the Midlands and one each from Eastern, Western, Scottish and Irish tournaments. The whole structure was in place by July. The 1910 finals were played at Bushey Hall, starting on October 19th, and, like the *News of the World* Tournament, it was a match play event. W.L. Ritchie defeated Willie Watt in the final by 5 and 4. Ritchie was Braid's assistant, and it was perhaps only fitting that he should win in the year of his master's last triumph in the Open. Ritchie won £21 and Watt £10.50. In the presentation speeches, W.J. Todd of

A group of professional golfers in 1896. They include Sandy Herd, J.H. Taylor, Harry Vardon, James Braid and Ben Sayers.

Perrier offered a purse of £50 for Ritchie to play the winner of the *News of the World* Tournament, James Sherlock. Sherlock subsequently declined the challenge.

There were two major format changes in 1911. The finals were 36 holes of stroke play, and 20 players qualified for this rather than 16. C. Macey of Crowborough finished one stroke ahead of A. Simpson in the 1911 final, held on October 18th at Burhill. The 1912 final was at West Middlesex, on October 17th, and was won by W.E. Brown of Stoke Poges. The 1913 final was at Totteridge, on October 16th, and was won by F.C. Jewell. In 1914 only the Southern section qualifying competition had been played before the outbreak of war.

Although the tournament was advertised as having 100 guineas in prizes, only £84 was paid out in cash to the players. £10.50 was given to the employer of the winning assistant, and £10.50 was "devoted to printing and other attendant expenses". In 1910 prizes were given to all 16 players who reached the final. The losing semifinalists received £5.25 each, the losing quarter-finalists £4.20 each and the first round losers £3.15 each. When the format switched to stroke play, 20 players qualified for the final, and the winner received £20, the runner-up £10, third and fourth place

£5 each, fifth to 10th £4 each and 11th to 20th £2 each.

Harold Hilton, writing about the 1910 final, was impressed by the speed at which the youngsters played: "I could not help thinking to myself that surely some of them must be hard-pressed to catch a train, or were afraid of missing an important appointment . . . and one could imagine George Duncan and his twin brother, if they were playing in front, causing some of the couples serious inconvenience by holding them up through their dilettantic methods."[6]

An article in *Golf Illustrated* in 1914 summed up the success of the tournament: "The object of the institution of the 'Perrier' Competition for Assistants, which was to allow the rising generation of professional golfers to show what mettle they were made of, has been strikingly vindicated, all four winners of the event to date having secured good positions . . . There is no doubt that this event is a genuine 'hidden talent' competition."[7]

The London Foursomes Tournament

This tournament, which was played under varying guises between 1906 and 1911, perfectly illustrated the changing nature of tournament golf in this period. It began as a pro-am event, became an independent professional tournament for the Dewar Shield, and then came under the control of the PGA. It was eventually superseded by the *Sphere* and *Tatler* cups and was a competition constantly dogged by controversy.

The saga began in February 1906, when the committee of Walton Heath Golf Club took it upon themselves to organise a foursomes tournament for London clubs. The conditions were that each club could enter only one team, and that team could consist of either two amateurs, or one amateur and one professional. The field was quite strong, with Braid, Taylor, Batley, Hepburn, Alfred Toogood, W. Hunter, Wilfrid Reid and James Kinnell all representing their clubs with an amateur partner. Not surprisingly, Mid-Surrey, with Taylor and Sidney Fry, and Walton Heath, with Braid and Herbert Fowler, reached the finals. What was surprising was that the Mid-Surrey team won the tournament by an emphatic 9 and 8 over their opponents' own course, which had been designed by Fowler.

The pro-am format immediately caused a great deal of controversy. Before a single shot had been played, a letter signed by "Pure Sport" appeared in the March 2nd *Golf Illustrated*. The writer opposed the inclusion of professionals in the event, because "nothing but harm to the game can result from this close association of amateurs in public competition with professionals who make their living by playing." Two weeks later another letter signed with a pen name, this time "Amateur", appeared, expressing great concern that amateurs were competing in a competition with, and against, professionals on an equal footing, and that the conditions for the tournament "showed an entire lack of appreciation of what is involved in the amateur status". The following week "A Conservative" went further and said that the format of the tournament threatened the destruction of the social element in golf. George Riddell wrote to *Golf Illustrated* to refute the criticisms levelled at his club. He observed that "one of the merits of true sport is the friendly spirit and camaraderie which it engenders between different classes," and that members of the Royal family and leading politicians often played in foursomes with professionals. "As far as I can ascertain no decadence has yet been apparent in the manners or conduct of the distinguished amateurs who have taken part in these foursomes."

Even a figure as powerful as Riddell failed to quell all the uneasiness about the format of the tournament, and, in July 1906, the clubs at Sunningdale, Woking and Byfleet announced that they were going to sponsor a London Foursomes tournament for amateurs only. In August, the Walton Heath Club joined the committee of the other three clubs and abandoned their own foursomes competition. In December, it was announced that there would be a London foursomes tournament for professionals only. None of the Triumvirate entered the new tournament, which began in January 1907, and the final was scheduled for February 27th at Bramshot.

As the team of Rowland Jones and Alfred Toogood progressed through the rounds, a new problem surfaced. Jones was booked to go on the French tour with Braid, Taylor, Herd, Sayers, White, Ray and both Vardons, and would not be available to play the final on the stipulated date. They were due to meet P.J. and E.P. Gaudin in the quarter-final, but the latter had to scratch when P.J. Gaudin became ill and was unable to play the match by the required date. They then had an easy 8 and 7 win over J. Turner and R. McKenzie in the semifinal, while Ralph Smith and Albert Tingey won their match against Reid and A. Hallam.

Now the fun began. Jones asked that the final be postponed until March 6th – after his return from France. Smith and Tingey objected, and claimed a walkover victory. Smith, in a long and articulate letter to *Golf Illustrated*, written on February 26th, explained that it was a matter of principle. After all, the precedent had been set by Jones himself, when he claimed a victory over the Gaudins in the quarter-final when the brothers were unable to play the match by the stipulated date. He argued that Jones, knowing that he would not be able to play on the date of the final, should have scratched. Jones wrote an equally long defence of his actions, and said that he had been told that the majority of players in the tournament had agreed to postpone the final until March 6th, and that only Smith and Tingey had objected. In the end, Smith and Tingey were awarded the victory, after what *Golf Illustrated* called "a somewhat acrimonious and certainly unedifying dispute between the finalists". The writer went on to say that this could have all been avoided if the tournament had been held "under the auspices of a recognised club or body," and that Vardon, Braid and Taylor had been very wise not to have entered.

Despite all this, the tournament was held again the next year, with the first round kicking off on March 3rd, 1908, at Banstead Downs. The semifinals were played on March 31st, and White and Ben Sayers Junior routed the holders, Smith and Tingey, by 11 and 10, while Mayo and Duncan beat Wynne and Frostick. The final was scheduled for the following Tuesday. Once again the final failed to take place, as Jack White fell ill again, and could not play. Although Duncan and Mayo offered to postpone the final, the committee of management, "bearing in mind last year's disagreement", awarded them first place.

The tournament took place again in 1909, but was now under the control of the Southern section of the PGA. The rounds through to the semifinal were played at Bushey Hall, on April 6th and 7th. Batley and W. Horne scored a major upset, defeating J.H. and Joshua Taylor in the semifinal by a score of 5 and 3. The final was not played until the end of May – but at least it was actually played. Batley and Horne defeated James Bradbeer and G. Charles by 11 and 10.

The 1910 competition was scheduled for January 26th, 27th and 28th, at Stoke Poges. Bad weather hindered the play, and the final had to be postponed for ten days. The Taylor brothers then defeated the holders, Bradbeer and Charles, by 6 and 5. The 1911 competition was played at Fulwell from March 14th to 16th, and actually finished on schedule. The Taylors were defeated in the second round by Duncan and Mayo, who were in turn beaten in the semifinals by Charles Johns and A. Kettley. Fred

Robson and Tom Ball won the other semifinal, and went on to win the final by 3 and 2.

With the establishment of the *Sphere* and *Tatler* cups as a national foursomes competition in 1911, no further Dewar Shield tournaments were held. It is highly significant that the tournament ran smoothly only after its management was taken over by the PGA in 1909.

NOTES

1. The number of players qualifying from each region for *The News of the World* Tournament was as follows:

Section	Year and Number											
	1903	1904	1905	1906	1907	1908	1909	1910	1911	1912	1913	1914
Irish	2	2	2	2	2	2	2	1	1	1	1	1
Scottish	4	3	3	3	4	4	4	2	2	2	2	2
Northern	5	6	5	5	6	7	7	7	7	7	7	7
Midland	5	5	5	5	4	4	4	4	5	5	5	5
Southern	16	16	16	16	14	14	13	13	12	2	12	12
Welsh			1	1	2	1	1	2	2	2	2	2
Western							1	2	2	2	2	2
Eastern								1	1	1	1	1
TOTAL	32	32	32	32	32	32	32	32	32	32	32	32

2. *Golf Illustrated*, October 25th, 1907
3. *My Golfing Life*, Harry Vardon, 1933
4. The number of players qualifying from each section for the *Sphere* and *Tatler* cups between 1911 and 1914 was as follows:

	1911	1912	1913	1914
Southern	24	24	24	26
Northern	14	14	14	14
Midlands	9	9	10	9
Western	5	4	3	3
Eastern	3	2	2	2
Scottish	4	5	5	5
Welsh	3	4	4	3
Irish	2	2	2	2
Total	64	64	64	64

5. *Golf Illustrated*, May 29th, 1914
6. *Golf Illustrated*, October 28th, 1910
7. *Golf Illustrated*, April 3rd, 1914

9. European Opens

The French Open

THE FIRST FRENCH OPEN WAS PLAYED ON JULY 1ST AND 2ND, 1906, over the La Boulie course at Versailles, outside Paris. From the start it was a 72-hole event played over two days. There were six prizes offered, ranging from £50 for the winner down to £6. British entrants included Tom Vardon, Ray, Reid, Kinnell and Ernest Gray, but Arnaud Massy was the winner. His 292 was 11 strokes better than the runner-up, Tom Vardon.

La Boulie also hosted the 1907 French Open, on June 29th and 30th. British honour was perceived as being at stake, after Massy had won the Open at Hoylake. A reporter in the July 5th, 1907, *Golf Illustrated* wrote: "[Massy's] victory, well received as it was in this country, had nevertheless the natural effect of inciting our defeated champions to obtain their revenge at the first opportunity." Both Vardons, Braid (a notoriously poor sailor who was sea-sick with the least provocation), Duncan, Ray, Kinnell, Mayo and Wilfrid Reid all ventured to La Boulie. Not only did Massy win again, but Jean Gassiat, "another Biarritz product, a player little known in this country, and who has never competed in the Open Championship," finished second. Massy's winning score was 298, and the best British effort was Braid's, on 301. Reid, Vardon, Duncan and Ray were all on 308.

British honour was restored in 1908, again at La Boulie, on June 28th and 29th. The Triumvirate all returned, along with Tom Vardon, Mayo, Sayers and Reid. Taylor became the first British winner, finishing on 300, while Massy and Mayo tied for second, four shots behind.

The Triumvirate filled the top three spots in 1909, once again at La Boulie, on June 17th and 18th. After the first 36 holes, Taylor was four strokes behind Braid, who was tied for the lead with Maurice Dauge, on 146. The next day Taylor could do no wrong, and played the last two rounds in 71 and 72, for a total of 293. This left Braid needing a 74 in the final round to tie, but the Scotsman's long putt at the last hole refused to go down, and he finished second by a stroke. Vardon was third and Maurice Dauge was fourth, while Massy could manage only a tie for seventh place with Mayo. British professionals occupied eight of the top ten places.

Braid made it three British winners in a row at La Boulie in 1910, when

J. Douglas Edgar.

his last round of 72 enabled him to finish two strokes ahead of Massy. Vardon was a further two shots behind, and Taylor was in only 11th place, 15 strokes off the pace. Again, there were eight British professionals in the top ten places. In 1911 at La Boulie, on July 3rd and 4th, Massy made up for his disappointing play-off in the Open by romping through the field, finishing seven strokes ahead of Ted Ray, eight ahead of Mayo and nine better than Vardon. Taylor was a disappointing 10th.

All the leading British players were present at La Boulie at the beginning of July for the 1912 French Open. Jean Gassiat finished a stroke ahead of Vardon, whose 10-foot putt for the tie just missed. Tellier was third and Ray was fourth. In fifth place was the American Open champion, J.J. McDermott; Taylor, Massy, Duncan and Braid all finished well down the list.

The prize money at the French Open was about the same as that for the British Open, allowing for currency conversion. It totalled about £130, with £50 for the winner. In January 1913, the leading British players were concerned with the spread of the money. It was claimed that, with the exception of the first three, "all other prize winners are considerably out of pocket after attending the meeting." The next month, *Golf Illustrated* reported: "In response to the request signed by leading British professionals, the Union de Golf de France has generously consented to add seven more prizes to the existing eight in the French Open Championship. The new prizes will consist of three of £6 each and four of £5 each."[1] This brought the total purse to 4,000 francs, or £160.

There was a new location, and a new time of the year, for the 1913 French Open: it was played at Chantilly, on October 13th and 14th. George Duncan was six strokes behind after the first day, but rallied brilliantly on the second, with a 73 and a 74, for a total of 304. As usual, he was long off the tee, but the key lay in his excellent approach shots. His putting was only average, which cost him the chance for record scores. In the end he finished three shots better than Braid, and four ahead of Sherlock. In his report on the match in *Golf Illustrated*, C.B. Macfarlane wrote: "There are many championships nowadays, but the French is regarded as one of the most important of the year. It always attracts a good field and at Chantilly last week there was one of the strongest that has ever met to dispute the possession of the title."[2]

A record 88 players entered at Le Touquet, on July 6th and 7th, 1914. It was a tournament of upsets. Massy did the best of any of the French players, finishing 14th. An amateur, H.D. Gillies, from Woking, finished fifth. But the biggest surprise was the winner, the unheralded J. Douglas Edgar from the Northumberland Golf Club, who finished six strokes ahead of Vardon. He played a strong all-round game on the day, while Vardon's usual problem with putting in the second and third rounds stopped him from making a run for the title. It is no small wonder that the editorial in *Golfing* carried the headline: "The Shock of the Season."[3]

The Belgian Open

The Belgian Open was first played in 1910, at the Royal Golf Club de Belgique, Brussels, and was a 36-hole championship that offered less money and attracted fewer entries than the French Open. Prize money in 1910 totalled £84, and was distributed among the top eight players. In 1911 this went down to £67.50, split among the top five players. For the next three years, £100 was paid out to the top ten finishers. With the exception of 1911, this event tended to be held just after the French Open. The Belgian golf federation was advised in 1913 that, "unless it was played the same week as the French, a separate journey would be entailed and the entry would be sure to suffer".[4] The entry for the 1910 Belgian Open is described as "practically the same as for the French Championship".[5]

Both Vardons, Herd, Williamson, Rowland Jones, Braid and Sherlock all

George Duncan in 1910.

competed in the 1910 Belgian Open. Massy won, finishing five shots ahead of Vardon and Herd, and eight better than Tom Vardon. Braid, Jones, Williamson and Sherlock were all nine strokes behind. In 1911, Charles Mayo finished three strokes ahead of Massy, and five ahead of Jones, in Brussels, again on May 31st.

A much stronger field was in evidence for the 1912 Belgian Open, at Knocke on July 5th. Duncan, Ray and Tom Ball finished the regulation 36 holes tied on 144. The players were given the choice of holding the 18-hole play-off that evening or the next day. As they all had imminent engagements in England, they opted to play that same day. Ball was never in it, and finished on 78. Meanwhile, Duncan and Ray were tied after 16 holes. Duncan found a bunker with his second shot, while Ray had an easy shot to the green. Duncan blasted out of the bunker and on to the green, while Ray left his approach short. Duncan sank his long putt, and Ray did not . . . and that was the difference. Duncan finished on 70, one stroke ahead of Ray. Braid was fourth, Taylor fifth and Gassiat seventh; Vardon finished out of the money, and Massy did not compete. By the time of the

1913 Belgian Open at Lombartzyde, on October 16th, Vardon and Ray were in America, but otherwise "the cream of professional golfers" competed for the championship.[6] Braid did the first round in 71, to take a two shot lead over Tom Ball and Rowland Jones. Braid's play began to fall apart at the 7th hole, when he took three putts, and then at the 8th, when he failed to clear a bunker and took six. His putting touch then took an early boat back to England, and he finished the round in 75. With the soft greens enabling Ball to pitch right up to the pin and bite, he had tied Braid by the 12th hole. Ball arrived at the 18th needing to play the last in five or less to win. His approach shot, a pitch to the green, shot five yards past the hole, and his putt went three feet past the hole in the other direction. His fourth shot of the hole reached the edge of the hole, but refused to dive down. He tapped in, to win the tournament, a stroke ahead of Braid, and two ahead of Gassiat. Ball then successfully defended his title in 1914, when only eight British-based players competed, at Antwerp, on July 11th. The entrants included British professionals based in Spain, Belgium, Germany, France and Holland. Charles Mayo finished second, four strokes behind, with Rowland Jones third.

The German Open

The German Open was played for only two years, and was highly controversial. The tournament was first held in 1911, and was styled "The Open Professional Tournament at Baden-Baden". It had a total purse of £240, with £100 going to the winner. There was a strong field, that included Vardon, Ray, Herd, Reid, Tom Ball, Mayo and Gassiat. Vardon won easily, with a 72-hole competition record score of 279, to finish nine strokes clear of Herd.

At the conclusion of the event, a meeting was held at which "it was decided that the Baden-Baden Club should secede from the German Golf Union, and hold another similar competition next year under the title of the Open Championship of Germany. The Baden-Baden Club resents the recent action of the Golf Union in forbidding them to use the National Championship title for their competition, and they say that as the Baden-Baden course is the only 18-hole course in Germany, it is the proper venue for the National Championship."[7] The prize money was to be increased to £500. The report finished with the words "The action of the German Golf Union will be awaited with interest."

On September 1st, *Golf Illustrated* published the formal announcement of the 1912 Open Championship of Germany. The tournament was endorsed by the leading British players who had been in Baden-Baden. Needless to say, the German Golf Union objected to the club's plans, and its secretary sent a letter of protest to *Golf Illustrated*, published on September 15th, 1911. The Union, founded in 1907, had considered whether to hold an Open competition, but "the delegates have clearly ascertained that such a first-class competition would be premature for the still very young and just developing game [in Germany] and would entail a burden which it is as yet not in a position to bear". Herr Wentzel, of the German Golf Union, felt that "The Baden-Baden committee is in no way in a position to have the most elementary conception of how to distinguish between 'open' and 'restricted'." The dispute continued, but did not deter the committee of the Baden-Baden club, and the 1912 Open Championship of Germany went ahead without the sanction of the German Golf Union.

The championship offered a total purse of £500, the largest sum ever given for a tournament in Europe, and £100 more than the *News of the World* Tournament in England. First prize was £100, second £80, third £60, fourth £45, fifth £30, sixth £20, and seventh, eighth, ninth and tenth £15 each. With rewards like that at stake, all the leading British professionals entered, with the single exception of Braid. Taylor and Ray tied for first after 72 holes, with 279, the same score as Vardon the previous year. The play-off was over nine holes. Taylor completed these in an astounding score of 28, to defeat Ray by six strokes. W.H. Horne was third, Duncan fourth, Vardon fifth and Tom Ball sixth.

In July 1913, the Baden-Baden Club announced that they were suspending "the holding of the Open Championship of Germany over their course until the work of reconstruction at present in hand is completed". The course would be ready and the championship resumed in 1915. World events soon made the dispute between the club and their union irrelevant.

NOTES
1. *Golf Illustrated*, February 23rd, 1913
2. *Golf Illustrated*, October 24th, 1913
3. *Golfing*, July 15th, 1914
4. *Golf Illustrated*, March 14th, 1913
5. *Golf Illustrated*, June 10th, 1910
6. *Golfing*, October 22nd, 1913
7. *Golf Illustrated*, August 25th, 1911

Epilogue

WORLD WAR I BEGAN ON AUGUST 4TH, 1914. The whole country went on an immediate wartime footing, and many sports cancelled all their fixtures. Golf was no exception. The August 19th edition of *Golfing* announced that all the tournaments organised by the PGA were cancelled. This included the *News of the World* Tournament and the Perrier Assistants' Tournament. Unions, and clubs followed suit and cancelled their competitions. The only event that was to go ahead was the International, with all the proceeds going to the Prince of Wales' Fund (war relief). This arrangement was dropped a month later, and the match cancelled. The first British golfer to die in the war was William Douglas, son of the greenkeeper at Aberdeen, and a player of some ability.

The war brought an era to an abrupt end. There was to be no more competitive professional golf until 1919. Any age in history only becomes "golden" retrospectively, and the period 1894 to 1914 is no exception. It is often referred to as a "golden age" for both golf and cricket, and is viewed as one long Victorian and Edwardian country-house weekend. In reality, like any 21-year period, there was social unrest, economic crisis and international tensions and wars. The number of workers who belonged to unions increased from 1,559,000 in 1893 to 4,145,000 in 1914, and the Trade Disputes Act of 1906 clarified the legal status of trade unions. In turn, increasing labour unrest was matched by the growth of the Labour Party, which returned 53 members in the 1906 election. At the other end of the social scale, there was a clash between the House of Commons and the House of Lords over the 1909 budget which threatened the very being of the Upper House. There were problems in Ireland, problems in the Balkans and various economic crises. In short it was business as usual in the cycle of an industrialized society.

Occasionally some of these problems spilled over on to the golf course. "A Golfers Fund for the Widows and Orphans of those who Fall in the Transvaal War" was established by *Golf Illustrated* in 1899, aided by a "Golf Professionals' War Fund", the work of J.H. Taylor. Taylor proposed that players should donate money to the fund. According to the list published in *Golf Illustrated*, Taylor donated £1, Braid 50p, White 50p, Peter McEwan £1, David McEwan 50p, Willie Aveston 50p, Walter Toogood 25p, the

A.J. Balfour contemplates a putt.

Midland Professional Golf Club £1 and various others between 25p and 50p.[1] This paled in comparison with the £1,155 raised by the amateurs for the Officers' Branch of the War Fund, or the £1,450 raised for the Freddie Tait Memorial Fund, after his death in action. The gulf between the professionals' efforts and those of the amateurs was economic, not moral. Later, in response to the sinking of the *Titanic* in 1912, the PGA gave £10.50 to the *Daily Telegraph Titanic* Relief Fund.[2]

The suffragettes' campaign caused problems for golf clubs. In 1909, H.H. Asquith needed six policemen to protect him from the suffragettes when he played golf at Hythe that September. The threat to golf courses by the suffragettes campaigning for votes for women was very real. In 1913 a club secretary could purchase insurance from Lloyds of London to cover any damage done to the club or course by the suffragettes or merely damage to the greens. The R & A insured the Old and New Courses in St Andrews for £1,000 each against damage by suffragettes from April to December 1913. Damage did occur to golf clubs and courses. Typical of the problem, the club at Bath was attacked in March 1914, and three greens were badly mutilated and "the usual labels inscribed 'Votes for Women' were tied to the flags."[3]

With the tremendous growth of the game between 1894 and 1914, golf had become big business. An article in *Golf Illustrated* in 1911 pointed out that "Every year sees an increase in the number of courses all over the world, and the business side of golf has now become an undertaking affecting many huge financial concerns." It observed this effect on the Open

Championship itself: "Nowadays there are two sides to the Open, the playing and the business – in fact, it might be safely said that, though the former is *the* side, the latter is perhaps the more important side."[4]

Nevertheless, whether it was "golden" or not, the period from 1894 to 1914 had revolutionised professional golf. By the end of it, players could compete on a far more regular basis in tournaments in both Britain and Europe, thus giving them a greater opportunity to make a name for them-

The Rt. Hon. A.J. Balfour, M.P.

Douglas Rolland putting against J.H. Taylor at Sandwich.

selves and win prize money and/or secure a better club appointment. The formation of the PGA was the catalyst for these changes. Indeed the foundations of the way professionals competed in tournaments up to the coming of television in the 1960s were laid in this period.

NOTES
1. *Golf Illustrated*, February 23rd, 1900
2. *Golf Illustrated*, May 17th, 1912
3. *Golf Illustrated*, March 13th, 1914
4. *Golf Illustrated*, July 14th, 1911

Appendices

1. Exhibition Matches

This appendix looks at how the leading professionals performed against one another and against other professionals in exhibition match play.

Because of the different formats, and the varying quality of opposition, I devised a simple point-scoring system to enable like to be compared with like for 13 players.

All opponents were divided into two groups – first-class and second-class players – and the matches were divided into the three classifications of singles, minis and foursomes. In singles, if a first-class player played another first-class player, the winner was awarded 8 points and the loser 0 points. They each received 4 points if they halved the match. If a first-class player played a second-class player, the first-class player received 3 points for a win, 1 point for a half and nothing if he lost.

It becomes somewhat more complicated for minis and foursomes. If a mini field contained at least two first-class players, the winner was given 8 points, the runner-up 4 points, the third-place finisher 1 point and the fourth 0 points. If there was a tie for first place, the joint winners had 6 points each. If there was only one first-class player in the field, the points are reduced. First place was worth 3 points, second place 2 points, third place 1 point and fourth place 0. In the event of a tie, the joint winners received 2 points each. In foursomes, if a team containing at least one first-class player defeated a team of two first-class players, each winner received 4 points and the losers 0 points. If the match was halved, all four players received 2 points. If a team containing at least one first-class player defeated a team consisting of one first-class player and one second-class player, or two second-class players, the winners received 2 points each and the losers 0 points. In the event of a halved match, all players received 1 point. As with all scoring systems, this is neither perfect nor foolproof, but I tried to apply it consistently and thus create a level playing-field.

The cumulative results of this system produced a few surprises. The top-ranked overall player in exhibition matches between 1894 and 1914 was James Braid, by a whisker over Ted Ray. All the averages were normally done to two decimal places, but it was necessary to go a third decimal place to find the winner: Braid had a point average of 3.070 and Ray had one of 3.068. The full results are in Table 3.

Table 1. Point Averages of Leading Players

Name	Events	Points	Average
James Braid	526	1,615	3.070
Ted Ray	177	543	3.068
Harry Vardon	544	1,602	2.9
George Duncan	187	531	2.84
Arnaud Massy	74	205	2.77
Charles Mayo	44	121	2.75
J.H. Taylor	529	1,450	2.74
Sandy Herd	281	764	2.72
Tom Ball	57	152	2.67
Fred Robson	24	64	2.67
Andrew Kirkaldy	98	239	2.44
Ben Sayers	116	205	1.77
Jack White	109	170	1.56

Ray did not play his first match until 1901, when he was still only 24, and Duncan not until 1902, when he was 19. Massy began playing in Britain in the same year. Mayo, Ball and Robson were viewed as the rising stars late in the period. Mayo began playing important matches in 1906, and both Ball and Robson in 1908. Robson was then felled by illness, which limited his participation after 1910. Sayers and Kirkaldy both played throughout the period, but were most active before the turn of the century. Jack White was building up his career when his health gave way, shortly after he won the Open in 1904. His performances tailed off dramatically after that.

Table 2. Singles Matches Point Averages

Name	Events	Average
Ball	14	4.50
Ray	74	4.42
Mayo	21	4.24
Robson	10	4.20
Braid	226	3.78
Vardon	253	3.72
Taylor	239	3.58
Herd	129	3.22
Duncan	84	2.85
Massy	28	2.75
Kirkaldy	60	2.48
Sayers	70	2.17
White	59	2.07

Obviously Ball, Mayo and Robson played relatively few matches. The most interesting statistics are those which show how much higher Ray's average was than any member of the Triumvirate, and how close Braid's and Vardon's averages were.

Table 3. Foursomes Point Average

Name	Events	Average
Massy	30	1.87
Herd	98	1.745
Braid	197	1.736
Mayo	19	1.63
Ball	29	1.52
Kirkaldy	24	1.50

Table 3 (cont.)

Name	Events	Average
Vardon	195	1.49
Ray	75	1.48
Duncan	74	1.41
Taylor	196	1.33
Robson	10	1.20
White	12	1.03
Sayers	13	0.94

There are several surprises here. One is how relatively low Taylor ranks as a foursomes player compared with his peers. Another is how well Massy did, and how close Herd and Braid were. Duncan and Mayo were a highly-rated team – and it is interesting to see the differential in their averages. Ray's final position is not too surprising; he had the reputation of putting his partner in parts of the course that most players never visited.

Table 4. Mini Event Point Averages

Name	Events	Average
Massy	16	4.50
Braid	103	4.06
Duncan	29	3.97
Kirkaldy	14	3.86
Vardon	96	3.85
Ray	28	3.75
Taylor	94	3.56
Herd	54	3.30
Ball	14	3.21
Robson	4	2.50
Sayers	13	1.77
White	16	0.81
Mayo	4	0.25

It is interesting that Massy is once again top of the table, but he played in relatively few events. Braid had a clear advantage over Vardon and Taylor, and Duncan did very well.

Of the players under review, Vardon, Taylor, Braid and Herd were the only four who were in their prime throughout the entire period, and it is worth looking at their annual averages. In those years in which he played at least ten matches in Britain or Europe, the highest average Vardon ever achieved was 3.83 in 1899. The best Taylor ever did was in 1895, when his average was 3.71, but he accomplished this before the full advent of Vardon and Braid. Given Braid's reputation for dominating golf between 1901 and 1910, it is most interesting to discover that his two best seasons (albeit when he played only 16 matches in both years) were 1897 and 1898, when he averaged 5.19 and 4.50 respectively. His best year when he played more than 20 matches was 1906, when he averaged 4.46, the highest for a year in which a player took part in more than 20 matches. Sandy Herd had his best year in 1896, with 5.29, but he played only 14 matches.

On the other side of the coin, Vardon's worst years were, surprisingly, not those following his ill-health in 1903, but 1898, with 2.23 in 13 matches, and 1909, when he managed just 2.36 in 25 matches. Taylor's worst years were 1911, with 1.53 in 30 matches, and 1897 – 2.00 in 15 matches. Braid's two worst years, when he played more than 10 matches, were 1913 and 1912, when he averaged 1.61 in 28 matches and 2.05 in 37 matches respectively, and was plagued with eye problems. Herd's two worst seasons, when he played more than 10 matches, were 1911 and 1909, with 1.64 and 1.63, in 19 and 11 matches respectively.

Table 5. Annual Leading Point Average 10 Matches or more

Year	Player	Average
1894	Rolland	3.39
1895	Taylor	3.71
1896	Herd	5.29
1897	Braid	5.19
1898	Braid	4.50
1899	Vardon	3.83
1900	Braid	2.91
1901	Vardon	3.21
1902	Vardon	3.72
1903	Vardon	3.58
1904	Taylor	3.44
1905	Vardon	3.45
1906	Braid	4.46
1907	Massy	4.70

Table 5 (cont.)

Year	Player	Average
1908	Braid	3.77
1909	Braid	3.79
1910	Duncan	3.52
1911	Braid	3.45
1912	Duncan	3.62
191	Duncan	3.29
1914	Ray	3.61

As Braid had the best average of any player, it is not surprising that he leads the table the most times – seven. What is surprising is that he did so as early as 1897. Vardon had the best average five times between 1899 and 1905. The extent of his supremacy in those years can be seen by the fact that the two years that he did not finish with the best average were 1900, when he spent most of the year in America, and 1904, when he was still recovering from his physical collapse of the previous year. George Duncan had the best average three times, which makes his failure to win the Open before 1914 all the more surprising. Conversely Taylor, a five-time Open champion, only had the best average twice. Ray, Massy and Herd all led once, as did Douglas Rolland. Rolland had a spectacular season in 1894, accruing 61 points in 18 matches, but he did not last long – he moved south, was injured and played in only four matches the next season, winning a total of four points.

2. Tournaments

As with exhibition matches, I have devised a simple point-scoring system, so that it is possible to compare the careers of the leading professionals on a like-for-like basis. I considered using the Sony ranking system, but that is too complicated for the size and nature of tournaments in the period under review. The sizes of the fields were obviously much smaller than those today, or indeed even than in the inter-war period. The system also had to be able to deal with the fact that 21% of the tournaments were either match play or a split format. As has been shown, the split format was particularly popular in major independent tournaments and both the *News of the World* and the *Sphere* and *Tatler* Cups finals were match play. Therefore, in the end, the same number of points needed to be awarded for third- and fourth-place finishes, and an equal number for finishing fifth, sixth, seventh and eighth.

Tournaments were divided into two categories, major and other. The majors were the Open, the *News of the World*, the *Sphere* and *Tatler*, the French Open, the Belgian Open, the US Open and the German Open. A tournament with a confirmed field of at least 32, and a total purse of over £100, was considered by contemporary opinion to be truly significant. These were therefore classified as majors. The points awarded are outlined in Table 1.

Because of the relatively small fields, no points were awarded for finishing lower than eighth. Mine is neither the most sophisticated, nor perhaps even the fairest, system, but it was applied consistently and produces comparable results.

Table 1. Tournament Point Scoring System

Place	Major Tournament Points	Ordinary Tournament Points
1	15	12
2	10	8
3	8	6
4	8	6
5	4	3
6	4	3
7	4	3
8	4	3

Table 2. Point Averages of Leading Players

Name	Events	Points	Average
Vardon	153	1,167	7.63
Braid	147	1,042	7.09
Taylor	159	1,039	6.53
Ray	90	540	6.00
Duncan	75	439	5.85
Massy	49	281	5.73
Herd	164	932	5.68
White	83	248	2.99

Table 3. Players Rank by Tournament Wins

Name	Wins	Win %	1st or 2nd %
Vardon	52	34.0%	53.0%
Massy	12	24.5%	34.7%
Ray	21	23.3%	36.7%
Braid	34	23.1%	44.9%
Taylor	32	20.1%	40.3%

Open champions at St Andrews, from a painting by Michael Brown.

Table 3. (cont.)

Name	Wins	Win %	1st or 2nd %
Duncan	15	20.0%	28.0%
Herd	29	17.7%	30.5%
White	4	4.8%	10.8%

Table 4. Leading Point Average by Year

Year	Name	Average
1894	Herd	8.17
1895	Taylor	10.00
1896	Taylor	8.00
1897	Braid	7.80
1898	Vardon	11.83
1899	Vardon	12.40
1900	Vardon	*12.50
1901	Braid	9.44
1902	Vardon	8.44
1903	Vardon	10.38
1904	Taylor	7.89

Table 4. (cont.)

Year	Name	Average
1905	Braid	10.00
1906	Braid	9.83
1907	Massy	11.40
1908	Taylor	7.25
1909	Taylor	8.25
1910	Ray	6.78
1911	Vardon	8.45
1912	Ray	9.10
1913	Duncan	*8.67
1914	Vardon	8.14

* In 1900 none of the leading players participated in more than four tournaments. In 1913 Vardon had an average of 11.25, but played in only four ranking tournaments because of his tour of America.

One man clearly dominated tournament golf between 1894 and 1914 – Harry Vardon. In addition to the Triumvirate, I tracked the records of the other Open Champions in the period, plus

George Duncan. There were other players who achieved significant results and could have a higher average than White, but these would not have a meaningful impact on the overall picture.

These results show that the Triumvirate really did dominate tournament golf, and that Vardon was considerably better than the other two. This is reinforced when one looks at other measures. Vardon won 52 tournaments. Next came Braid with 34 wins, followed by Taylor with 32. This means that Vardon won 34% of all tournaments that he entered between 1894 and 1914. He finished second on 29 occasions, which means that he finished first or second in 53% of all events in which he played during those years.

However one looks at it, Vardon was head-and-shoulders above any of his contemporaries. The most points that Taylor earned in a year was 87, in 1908; Braid's best was 86, in 1902; Herd's best was 81, in 1895; and Ted Ray won 91 points in 1912. Vardon earned an astonishing 142 points in 1898, and also had the second highest total for a single year, with 93 in 1911. The only time Braid and Taylor averaged more than 10 points was in 1900, when they both played in only three tournaments. Arnaud Massy averaged 11.40 points in 1907. Ray's highest average was in 1912, and was 9.10; Herd's best was 9.00, in 1895, and Duncan's 8.67 in 1913. Vardon averaged over 10 points in a year five times: 1898, 1899, 1900, 1903 and 1913 (1900 was an anomaly, in that he entered only two point-earning tournaments that year).

Between May 4th, 1898 and June 5th, 1901, Vardon played in 22 tournaments. He won 17 and finished second the other five times. He reached the last eight at a tournament on June 12th, 1901, and then finished no worse than fourth until the first event of the 1904 season. In this second run he played 20 tournaments and won seven. He finished second six times, and third or fourth seven times. From 1898 to 1903 he averaged 10.37 points per tournament over 43 events. By comparison, in Braid's six best consecutive years (1901-1906), he averaged 8.78 points per tournament over 51 events. Vardon's dominance declined with the onset of illness, and he averaged only 5.77 points between 1904 and 1910. He then found form again, and averaged 8.06 points between 1911 and 1914.

In 1898 Vardon won ten tournaments. Braid, in his golden years, between 1901 and 1910, never won more than four tournaments in a year, which he did in 1903, 1905 and 1906. Taylor managed to win four tournaments in a year only once, in 1909, and won three in a year five times. Herd and Duncan were the only other two players to win more than four tournaments in year, aside from Vardon. They each won five, Herd in 1895 and Duncan in 1913.

The leading averages on an annual basis are based on a minimum of five tournaments (except 1900, when too few tournaments took place).

As to be expected, Vardon had the highest annual average seven times, followed by Taylor, who led on five occasions, to Braid's four. Ray led twice, and Herd, Massy and Duncan once each. What is surprising is that Taylor led the annual averages more than Braid, given that Braid had a cumulative average of 7.09 compared with Taylor's 6.53. Taylor's performance tailed off drastically after 1909. He averaged 4.21 points between 1910 and 1914, faring particularly poorly between 1910 and 1912, when his average was 3.5 points a year.

Of Vardon's 52 victories, 16 were in split format tournaments, three in match play tournaments and 33 in stroke play tournaments. In the stroke play events, three were won over 18 holes, one over 27 holes, 20 over 36 holes and nine over 72 holes. Of Taylor's 32 victories, three were in split-format tournaments, five in match play and 24 in stroke play. 16 of the latter were over 36 holes and eight over 72 holes. Braid won nine split-format tournaments, five match play events and 20 in stroke play, of which 12 were over 36 holes and eight were over 72 holes.

Herd won three split-format events, four match play tournaments and 22 at stroke play, of which one was over 18 holes, 19 over 36 holes and two over 72 holes. Ray won four match play tournaments, and 17 at stroke play. Two of these were over 18 holes, 14 over 36 holes and one over 72 holes. Duncan won one split-format tournament, two match play ones and 12 stroke play events. Two of these were 18-hole events, seven over 36 holes and three over 72 holes. Massy won two split-format tournaments and ten stroke play tournaments, of which six were 36-hole events and four were 72-hole.

Vardon shows a marked superiority in the split format tournaments, winning 16 of the 30 he entered, compared with three of 27 for Taylor, and nine of 27 for Braid. This did not carry over to straight match play tournaments. Here, Vardon won only three of the 18 he entered. He had more stroke play victories over 36 and 72 holes than any other player. Taylor and Braid were also competing in the same tournament in two-thirds of the total events Vardon entered. So he did not have a larger victory total because he played in softer events than any of the others. This is reflected in the point average difference.

3. Prize Money and Types of Events

For the purposes of this study, I looked at the earnings of eight specific players who won 41% of the total known tournament prize money available in the period. They were as follows:

Table 1. Prize Money Won by Eight Players

Name	Total £s	Average £s
Harry Vardon	1,749.85	19.66
James Braid	1,529.39	20.12
J.H. Taylor	1,503.83	18.80
Sandy Herd	1,319.43	14.34
George Duncan	756.85	22.26
Ted Ray	579.93	14.87
Arnaud Massy	493.50	24.68
Jack White	226.00	6.85

Over the 21 years, the total known prize money for both tournaments and exhibitions (excluding challenges) is £20,995.30. Coubrough, in his annual breakdown of tournaments and exhibitions for 1901 to 1912 (excluding 1905), gave an estimate of the total amount of prize money won in a year. Even allowing for the inclusion of challenge matches, his figures are higher than those given in reports of matches. Although they cannot be substantiated, they possibly give a better picture of the situation. He said that he was able to obtain additional figures by talking to the secretaries of clubs that held events. He gave figures in his summaries, but these are consistently less than his total figure, or the totals that I arrived at using the same written source material. The following table shows the figures that I have been able to find (excluding stated challenge purses), and compares them with Coubrough's annual totals (including challenge purses).

Table 2. Total Prize Money Won by Year, 1901-1912

Year	Known total £s	Coubrough's estimate £s
1901	960.00	2,094.00
1902	881.50	2,136.00
1903	714.00	1,800.00
1904	848.00	1,600.00
1905	997.00	
1906	646.00	1,700.00
1907	1,161.25	2,200.00
1908	1,270.50	3,500.00
1909	1,250.00	3,000.00+
1910	1,389.40	3,000.00+
1911	1,909.50	3,000.00+
1912	2,357.00	3,000.00+

Table 3. Total Tournament Prize Money, 1894-1914

Event Purses

Year	Amount Won	£25-£99	£100+
1894	489.50	7	1
1895	619.00	8	2
1896	802.00	8	4
1897	285.00	4	1
1898	621.00	8	2
1899	672.00	3	4

Table 3 (cont.)

Year	Amount Won	£25-£99	£100+
1900	261.75	3	1
1901	887.00	6	5
1902	737.50	6	3
1903	684.00	6	2
1904	808.00	6	4
1905	992.00	1	6
1906	646.00	6	2
1907	1,060.00	7	4
1908	1,151.00	7	5
1909	1,240.00	6	5
1910	1,385.40	9	6
1911	1,804.00	4	7
1912	2,357.00	7	10
1913	1,484.20	2	7
1914	935.00	2	5

Table 4. Events by Month of the Year

Month	Tournaments Total	Percentage	Exhibition Matches Total	Percentage
January	4	0.8%	22	1.3%
February	12	2.4%	29	1.9%
March	19	3.8%	82	4.9%
April	72	14.4%	198	11.9%
May	71	14.2%	260	15.6%
June	69	13.8%	195	11.7%
July	67	13.4%	220	13.2%
August	33	6.6%	182	10.9%
September	86	17.2%	151	9.1%
October	59	11.8%	171	10.3%
November	8	1.6%	115	6.9%
December	1	0.2%	42	2.5%
Total	501	100%	1,667	100%

Table 5. Types of Matches

Type	Total	Percentage
Singles	779	57.8%
Minis	176	13.1%
Foursomes	392	29.1%

Table 6. Format of Matches

Type	Total	Percentage
1. Singles		
Match Play	635	81.5%
Stroke Play	144	18.5%
2. Foursomes		
Two Ball	53	14.8%
Four Ball	304	85.2%

4. Growth of Golf Clubs

Table 1. Growth of All Types of Golf Clubs by Year

Year	New Clubs	Total Clubs
1885	14	161
1886	10	171
1887	31	202
1888	35	237
1889	53	290
1890	85	375
1891	104	479
1892	110	589
1893	127	716
1894	122	838
1895	121	959
1896	113	1,072
1897	81	1,153
1898	71	1,224
1899	52	1,276
1900	81	1,357
1901	61	1,418
1902	85	1,503
1903	110	1,613
1904	151	1,764
1905	175	1,939
1906	191	2,130
1907	174	2,304

Table 1. (cont.)

1908	152	2,456
1909	211*	2,667
1910	62*	2,729
1911	36	2,765
1912	34	2,799
1913	40	2,839
1914	5†	2,844

*Clubs appearing for the first time in the 1909/10 volume of *Golfing Annual* undated are listed as 1909.
†Partial year only.

Table 2. Geographic Spread of Ladies' Clubs in 1914

Country	Number
England	297
Scotland	121
Wales	20
Ireland	38
CI/IoM	3

Table 3. The Growth in the Number of Clubs with Courses Attached

Year	England	Scotland	Wales	Ireland	CI/IoM	Total
1889	106	85	2	9	0	106
1894	317	157	12	37	9	532
191	1,100	422	104	163	12	1,801

5. Results of Major Championships and Tournaments

Open Championships Winners

Year	Location	Advertised Purse	Total Purse Purse	Winner	Score
1894	Sandwich	£100	£90	J.H. Taylor	326
1895	St Andrews	£100	£90	J.H. Taylor	322
1896	Muirfield	£100	£90	Harry Vardon	316
1897	Hoylake	£100	£90	Harold Hilton	314
1898	Prestwick	£100	£90	Harry Vardon	307
1899	Sandwich	£100	£90	Harry Vardon	310
1900	St Andrews	£125	£115	J.H. Taylor	309
1901	Muirfield	£125	£115	James Braid	309
1902	Hoylake	£125	£115	Sandy Herd	307
1903	Prestwick	£125	£115	Harry Vardon	300
1904	Sandwich	£125	£115	Jack White	296
1905	St Andrews	£125	£115	James Braid	318
1906	Muirfield	£125	£115	James Braid	300
1907	Hoylake	£125	£115	Arnaud Massy	312
1908	Prestwick	£125	£115	James Braid	291
1909	Deal	£125	£115	J.H. Taylor	295
1910	St Andrews	£135	£125	James Braid	299
1911	Sandwich	£135	£125	Harry Vardon	303
1912	Muirfield	£135	£125	Ted Ray	295
1913	Hoylake	£135	£125	J.H. Taylor	304
1914	Prestwick	£135	£125	Harry Vardon	306

Sphere and *Tatler* Cups

Year	Location	Total Prize Money	Winner	Runner-up
1911	Walton Heath	£350	Sandy Herd, James Bradbeer	J.H. Taylor, W. Hambleton
1912	Hoylake	£350	George Duncan, James Sherlock	James Braid, C.T. Roberts
1913	Deal	£350	Harry Vardon, Tom Williamson	Joshua Taylor, B.F. James
1914	Sunningdale	£350	J.B. Batley	G.E. Smith

News of the World Tournament

Year	Location	Total Prize Money	Winner	Runner-up
1903	Sunningdale	£200	James Braid	Ted Ray
1904	Mid-Surrey	£240	J.H. Taylor	A.H. Togood
1905	Walton Heath	£240	James Braid	Tom Vardon
1906	Hollinwell	£240	Sandy Herd	Charles Mayo
1907	Sunningdale	£240	James Braid	J.H. Taylor
1908	Mid-Surrey	£240	J.H. Taylor	Fred Robson
1909	Walton Heath	£240	Tom Ball	Sandy Herd
1910	Sunningdale	£240	James Sherlock	George Duncan
1911	Walton Heath	£400	James Braid	Ted Ray
1912	Sunningdale	£400	Harry Vardon	Ted Ray
1913	Walton Heath	£400	George Duncan	James Braid

The French Open

Year	Location	Winner	Winning Score	Runner-up
1906	Paris	Arnaud Massy	292	Tom Vardon
1907	La Bouile	Arnaud Massy	298	Jean Gassiat
1908	La Bouile	J.H. Taylor	300	Arnaud Massy, Charles Mayo
1909	La Bouile	J.H. Taylor	293	James Braid
1910	La Bouile	James Braid	298	Arnaud Massy
1911	La Bouile	Arnaud Massy	284	Ted Ray
1912	La Bouile	Jean Gassiat	289	Harry Vardon
1913	Chantilly	George Duncan	304	James Braid
1914	Le Touquet	J.D. Edgar	288	Harry Vardon

The Belgian Open

Year	Location	Winner	Winning Score	Runner-up
1910	Royal Golf Club de Belgique	Arnaud Massy	139	Harry Vardon / Sandy Herd
1911	Brussels	Charles Mayo	144	Arnaud Massy
1912	Knocke	George Duncan	144	Ted Ray
1913	Lombartzyde	Tom Ball	145	James Braid
1914	Antwerp	Tom Ball	144	Charles Mayo

The German Open

Year	Location	Winner	Winning Score	Runner-up
1911	Baden-Baden	Harry Vardon	279	Sandy Herd
1912	Baden-Baden	J.H. Taylor	279	Ted Ray

Bibliography

Books
Adams, John *The Parks of Musselburgh,* Droitwich 1991
Barclay, J. *Golf in Canada – A History,* Toronto 1992
Braid, J. *Advanced Golf,* London 1908
Brailsford, D. *British Sport – A Social History,* Cambridge 1992
Colt, H.S. and Alison, C.H. *Some Essays on Golf Course Architecture,* Droitwich 1990
Cornish, G.S. and Whitten, R.E. *The Golf Course,* London 1981
Cousins, G. *Golf in Britain,* London 1975
Cousins, G. *Lords of the Links,* London 1977
Darwin, B. *British Golf,* London 1946
Darwin, B. *James Braid,* London 1952
Duncan, G. *Golf at the Gallop,* London 1951
Ensor, R. *England 1870-1914,* Oxford 1936
Girouard, M. *The Return to Camelot,* London 1981
Halford, D.G. *Old Lawn Mowers,* Shire Books 1982
Heathcote, C.G. *Tennis, Lawn Tennis, Racquets, Fives,* Badminton Library, 1903 edition
Henderson, I. and Stirk, D. *Golf in the Making,* Crawley 1979
Herd, A. *My Golfing Life,* London 1923
Hilton, H.H. *My Golfing Reminiscences,* London 1907
Hobbs, M. *British Open Champions,* London 1991
Holt, R. *Sport and the British,* Oxford 1990
Howell, A. *Harry Vardon,* London 1991
Hutchinson, H.G. *Golf,* Badminton Library, 1890
Hutchinson, H.G. *The Book of Golf and Golfers,* London 1899
Hutchinson, H.G. *The New Book of Golf,* London 1912
Hutchinson, H.G. *Fifty Years of Golf,* London 1919
Kirkaldy, A. *Fifty Years of Golf: My Memories,* London 1921
Kynaston, D. *Bobby Abel, Professional Batsman,* London 1982
Kynaston, D. *W.G.'s Birthday Party,* London 1990
Leach, H. *Great Golfers in the Making,* London 1907
Plumptre, G. *The Golden Age of Cricket,* London 1990
Ray, E. *Inland Golf,* London 1915
Ryde, P. *Royal & Ancient Championship Records 1860-1980,* St Andrews, 1981
Taylor, J.H. *Taylor on Golf,* London 1902
Taylor, J.H. *Golf: My Life's Work,* London 1943
Vamplew, W. *Play Up and Play the Game,* Cambridge 1988
Vardon, H. *The Complete Golfer,* London 1905
Vardon, H. *How to Play Golf,* London 1912
Vardon, H. *My Golfing Life,* London 1933
Viney, L. *The Royal & Ancient Book of Golf Records,* London 1991
Weaver, C. and Weaver, M. *Ransoms 1789-1989,* Ipswich 1989

Annual Publications
The Golfing Annual, Vol. I (1887/88) to Vol. XXIII (1909/10)
Nisbet's Golf Year Book, 1907, 1911, 1912, 1913, 1914

Weekly Publications
Golf, January 1894 to June 1899
Golf Illustrated, June 1899 to June 1914
Golfing, 1913 and 1914

Articles
Grieve, F.C. "Patents (1876-1904) in the British Golf Museum" – *Golfiana* Vol. 5 Number 1, 1993
Lewis, P.N. "The British & European 'Tour', 1906-1914" – *Golfiana* Vol. 4 Number 3, 1992
Lewis, P.N. "Prize Money for Pioneering Professionals – A Study of Tournaments and Exhibition Matches in Britain 1901-1904" – *Golfiana* Vol. 4 Number 1, 1992
Lewis, P.N. "Bounding Billy Bounces to Britain – The Arrival of the Rubber-Cored Ball" – *Golfiana* Vol. 3 Number 4, 1991
Lewis, P.N. "Mechanical Contrivances & Mallet Heads – Standardising Clubs in Britain 1907-1910" – *Golfiana* Vol. 3 Number 3, 1991

Archives
The Royal & Ancient Golf Club – Minutes of the Rules of Golf Committee
The Royal & Ancient Golf Club – Meetings of the Delegates of the Associated Clubs for the Open Championship
The Royal & Ancient Golf Club – Minutes of the Committee of Management and Business Meetings
The Royal & Ancient Golf Club – Minutes of the Green Committee

Index

Aberdeen 60
admission charges *see* gate-money
Aldeburgh 135
Amateur Championship 8, 98
    (1902) 20
    (1904) 28
    Ladies' (1902) 22
amateur status 36-38
amateur teams 54-55, 80-81, 89
Antwerp 153
appearance money 48, 78
Asquith, H.H. 156
Atlantic City, New Jersey 74
Auchterlonie, Willie 9, 16, 34, 36
    in Europe 80
Ayton, Laurie 89

Baden-Baden 153-154
Balfour, A.J. 13, 26, 156, 157
Ball, John 9, 21, 22, 36, 89, 91, 104, 106, 116, 121
Ball, S. 138
Ball, Tom 43, 45, 83, 87, 89, 90, 102, 115, 116, 117, 132, 133, 134, 135, 136, 142, 148, 152, 153, 154, 159-160
balls
    cost 16, 19, 20, 24
    gutta-percha v. rubber-cored 11, 17-30, 40
    feather 17
    rules 26-27
    selling by professionals 41
Bannister, Eric 134
Banstead Downs 142, 147
Bath 156
Batley, James B. 137, 138, 139, 143, 146, 147
Belgian Open Tournament 78, 83, 95, 98, 151-153, 171
Belgium 81
Blackpool 15, 96, 98
Blackwell, Edward 21
Bloxham, J. 138
Blyth, A.D. 36
Blyth, Hall 25
Bomboudiac, 81
Bournemouth 15, 26
Bradbeer, James 137, 147
Brady, Mike 92
Braid, James 9, 26, 27, 29, 33, 34, 40, 43, 45, 48, 49-50, 54, 55, 56, 58, 59, 61, 68, 69-70, 89, 92, 95, 96, 99, 100, 101, 102, 111
    background 31
    earnings 31, 44, 94, 166
    England *v.* Scotland matches 83, 84, 85, 86, 88, 90
    in Europe 81, 82, 83, 149, 150, 151, 152, 153
    London Foursomes 146, 147
    News of the World Tournament 130, 131, 132, 134, 135, 136
    on Haskell balls 22
    Open Championships 106-107, 109, 110, 111, 113, 114, 116, 118, 119, 120, 122, 126
    point averages 159-165
    Sphere and *Tatler* Cups 137, 139
    Tooting Bec Cup 140, 141, 142
    training 51
    see also Four Greens Foursome Match (1905)
Braid Hills, Edinburgh 92
Bramshot 96, 146
Brancaster 60
Brookline Country Club 76
Brown, David 9, 104
Brown, Vere 75
Brown, W.E. 144
Burhill 70, 71, 144
Burn, Captain 30
Burns, Jack 9
Bushey Hall 96, 98, 143, 147
Butchart, A.W. 97
Byfleet 146

caddies
    cost 16
Cagnes 82
Cairo 81
Callaway, 80, 81
Cann, George 76
Cannes 80, 81, 83
Catlin, A. 131
Cawsey, George 34, 87
Cawsey, H. 135
Challenge Cup 97
challenge matches 57-72
Championship of Lucerne 78
Chance Cup 97
Chantilly 83, 151
Charles, G. 81, 100, 147
Cheal, J. 139
Cinque Ports 116
    see also Deal
clothing 52-53
clubs (equipment)
    cost 16
    design 28, 30
    made and sold by professionals 38-39
clubs and societies 8
    cost of membership 16
    number 10, 11, 14-15, 28, 80, 168
Clucas, J. 97
Coburn, George 83, 84, 85, 86, 115, 130
Cockburn, B. 82
Collins, Fred 83, 84
Coltart, F. 88
Coronation Match 89
Costebelle 81, 82
costs of playing golf 16
    see also balls; clubs (equipment); clubs and societies
Country Life 90
County Down 96, 98
courses
    design 25, 32-33, 81
    number 10, 14-15
    on gentlemen's estates 35
Crowther, D.S. 51
Cruden Bay 96, 98
Cumming, George 75

Dauge, Maurice 82, 149
Deal 67-70, 88, 96, 116, 137
Deal Beach 78
Denham 143
Dewar Shield 145
Dingwell, John 76
Doig, Robert 81
Dorset 13
Douglas, Findlay 74
Douglas, William 155
Duncan, George 9, 27, 31-32, 43, 50, 51, 58, 68, 69, 70, 72, 92, 95, 102, 152
    earnings 166
    England *v.* Scotland matches 87, 88, 89, 90
    in America 78
    in Europe 83, 149, 150, 151, 152, 154
    London Foursomes 147
    News of the World Tournament 131, 132, 133, 134, 135
    Open Championships 118, 119-120, 122, 124
    point averages 159-164
    Sphere and *Tatler* Cups 137, 138, 139
    Tooting Bec Cup 142, 143
Dunn, Willie 74

Earlsferry 59
earnings 31-32, 38, 43-44, 74
    see also appearance money
Edgar, J. Douglas 150, 151
Edmundson, James 132
Edzell Tournament 96, 98, 99
Egan, Walter 18
Egypt 81
Eltham 16
Engadine Club, Samaden 81
England *v.* Scotland matches 83-90
Essex County 76
Evans, Chick 78, 79, 89
exhibition matches 43-56

Fairhaven 16
Fergusson, Mure 25, 27, 28, 36
Fernie, R.S. 139

Fernie, Willie 8, 9, 34, 36, 59, 60, 61
   England v. Scotland matches 83, 84, 85
   Open Championships 106
Findlay, Alexander 74
Four Greens Foursomes Match (1905) 47-48, 57, 64-68
Fowler, Herbert 146
Fox, 139
France 80-83
France v. US match (1913) 92
French Open Tournament 95, 98, 149-151, 170
Freemantle, 80
Frostick, F.H. 137, 147
Fry, Sidney 21, 146
Fulford, Harry 138
Fulford, W.H. 81
Fulwell 143, 147

Gadd, George 138, 139
Gammeter, J. 18
Ganton 31, 61, 62
Gassiat, Jean 81, 82, 83, 92, 149, 150, 152, 153
gate-money 47, 68
Gaudin, E.P. 142, 147
Gaudin, J.W. 137
Gaudin, P.J. 85, 86, 87, 88, 137, 143, 147
Gaudin, W.C. 83
Gentlemen v. Players match (1894) 36
German Golf Union 153, 154
German Open Tournament 95, 98, 153-154, 171
Germany 83
Gillies, H.D. 151
Glasgow North-Western 47
Golf Employment Bureau 39
Golf Professionals' War Fund 155
golfers, number of 15
Golfers Fund for the Widows and Orphans of those who Fall in the Transvaal War 155
Gordon Watney Challenge Cup 96
Graham, Jack 40
Graham, John 21, 22, 114
Grant, David 137
Gray, Ernest 85, 86, 116, 140, 142, 149
Gray, R.A. 137
green fees 16

Hallam, A.E. 138
Hambleton, W. 137
Hampshire, Isle of Wight and Channel Islands Association 98
Hampton Roads, Virginia 74
handicaps 100-102
Hanger Hill 140
Harlech 92
Harriman, H.M. 74
Haskell, Coburn 17
Haskell balls 17-30
Heliopolis 81
Helouan 81
Hepburn, James 83, 84, 85, 86, 88, 102, 131, 132, 133, 140, 146
Herd, Alex (Sandy) 9, 23, 26, 34, 40, 43, 45, 48, 58, 59, 60, 61, 67, 77, 92, 95, 99, 100, 102
   background 31
   earnings 44, 94, 166
   England v. Scotland matches 83, 84, 85, 86, 88, 89, 90
   in Europe 80, 81, 83, 152, 153
   London Foursomes 147
   News of the World Tournament 131, 133, 134, 135, 136
   on Haskell balls 22
   Open Championships 104-106, 110, 111, 112, 113, 116, 118, 120, 126
   point averages 159-165
   Sphere and Tatler Cups 137, 138, 139
   training 51
   see also Four Greens Foursome Match (1905)
Hezlet, Miss 22
Hilton, Harold 9, 18, 36, 106-107, 112, 120, 121
   on Haskell balls 27
   on younger players 145
holes, number of 15
Holland, Len 139
Hollinwell 131
Honourable Company of Edinburgh Golfers 103
   see also Muirfield
Horne, W. 147, 154
Hoylake 22, 36, 86, 89, 106, 110, 115, 137
Huddersfield 58
Hughes, Cyril 134
Hulton, Edward 57, 64
Hunter, W. 146
Huntercombe 62
Hutchings, Charles 20, 21, 36
Hutchinson, Horace 10, 11, 12, 15, 18, 36
   on Haskell balls 25
   on professionals 33
   on sales of balls by professionals 41
Hutchinson, Tom 75
Hutchison, Lt C. 40
Hutchison, Jock 78
Hyeres 81, 82
Hythe, 156

Ilkley 31
inland courses 15
Ireland v. Scotland matches 90
Irish Golf Union 97
Italy 82-83

James, B.F. 138, 139
Janion, Harold 124
Jefferies, W.T. 138
Jewell, F.C. 144
Johns, Charles 116, 117, 142, 147
Johnson, Frank 40
Jones, Rowland 37, 77, 102
   England v. Scotland matches 83, 84, 85, 86, 87, 90
   in Europe 81, 83, 151, 152, 153
   London Foursomes 146, 147
   News of the World Tournament 131
   Open Championships 113, 114
   Tooting Bec Cup 140, 141, 142, 143

Kay, James 83, 84, 85, 106
Kettley, A. 147
Kinloch, Frank 64
Kinnell, David 116
Kinnell, James 83, 84, 85, 86, 109, 113, 130, 146, 149
Kirkaldy, Andrew 9, 22, 34, 52, 58, 59, 60, 71, 72, 77, 82, 99, 112
   earnings 31
   England v. Scotland matches 85, 86, 88, 89
   News of the World Tournament 130
   Open Championships 104
   point average 159
Kirkaldy, Hugh 8
Kirkaldy, J. 86
knickerbockers 52-53
Knocke 152

La Boulie, Versailles 149
Ladies' Amateur Championship (1902) 22
Lafitte, A. 82, 92
Laidlay, John 61
Leaver, W. 137
Leeds Cup 97
Le Touquet 82, 151
Lewis, A.J. 138
Lewis, W.P. 137
links 15
Llangammarch Wells 71
Lloyd, Joe 76, 80
Lombartzyde, Belgium 81, 100, 153
London Foursomes 97, 145-148
London Pro-Am Foursomes 99
London Professionals Foursomes 99
Lonie, W.A. 141
Low, George 75
Low, John 68
   and Haskell balls 19, 24, 25
Lyon, George 75
Lytham 15, 98

McDermott, John J. 92, 121, 122, 124, 150
Macdougall, Gordon 75
McEwan, Douglas 31
McEwan, Peter 23
Macey, C. 144
Macfarlane, C.B. 151
McIntosh, C. 139
Mackenzie, R. 147
McLaren, J. 140
McNamara, Tom 92
McNeil, H. 137
mallet-headed clubs 28
Manchester Courier Cup 98
Manchester Open Tournament 98
Massy, Arnaud 9, 43, 44, 45, 68, 69-70, 81, 87, 89, 92, 102, 115

earnings 166
in Belgium 152
in France 81, 82, 83, 149, 150, 151
in Italy 82
News of the World Tournament 130
Open Championships 113, 115, 120
point averages 159-165
Matthews, A. 102
Maxwell, Robert 20, 21, 36, 61, 114, 121
Mayo, Charles H. 58, 68, 69, 70, 71, 87, 90, 97, 102, 128, 131, 132, 135, 138, 139, 142, 147, 152, 153, 159-160
Mentone 82
Mexico Country Club 77
Mid-Herts 131
Midland Challenge Cup 97
Midland Golf Association 39, 40
Midland Professional Foursomes 99
Midlands Counties 54
Midlands Golf Association 97
Mid-Surrey 62, 77, 96, 98, 130, 132, 134, 146
Mieville, Charles 40, 114, 126
Minchinhampton 58
Monte Carlo 82, 83
Montreux 81
Montrose 96, 98
Morris, Tom, Senior 33, 108
motor-cycles 13
Muirfield 89, 103, 106, 107, 110, 111, 114, 121, 125
Musselburgh 31, 59, 60
Musselburgh Open Tournament 96, 98, 99
Myopia Hunt Club 76

Nairn 47
Neasden 16, 142
Nevile, Miss 22
Newnes, George 57, 59
Newquay 64
News of the World Tournament 93, 94, 97, 98, 102, 129-136, 170
numbers of players 148
Nga Motu 28
Nice 81, 82, 83
Nicholls, Bernard 73, 74, 77
Nolan, T. 81
North Berwick 15, 58, 61, 62, 91, 95, 130
Northcliffe, Lord 78
Northern Counties Professional Golfers' Association 39
Northwood 140

Ockenden, James 126, 128
Oke, J. 102
Old Hall Manor 143
Olton Park front endpaper, 102
Open Championship 9, 36, 38, 94, 99, 103-128, 169
(1894) 104
(1895) 104-106
(1896) 106, 107
(1897) 106-108
(1898) 60, 61, 108
(1899) 108-109
(1900) 110
(1901) 110
(1902) 110-111
(1903) 111-112
(1904) 113
(1905) 113-114
(1906) 114
(1907) 115
(1908) 116
(1909) 116-117
(1910) 118, 119
(1911) 119
(1912) 121
(1913) 124
(1914) 127-128
and Haskell balls 26
courses 103, 116
entrance charges 103
exhibition tent 117, 125
organisation 8, 103-104, 112, 113, 114-116, 117, 119, 120 121, 124-128
prize money 7, 103, 107, 108-109, 110
Open Championship of Pennsylvania 78
Ormond, Florida 73, 74

Palm Beach, Florida 74, 77
Palmetto, Aiken, South Carolina 74
Park, John 81, 100
Park, Willie 8, 9, 45, 57, 58, 59, 60, 61, 62, 91, 100
England v. Scotland matches 83, 84, 85, 86, 90
in Europe 81
Open Championships 108, 109, 121
Park, Willie, Junior 33, 109
patents 11
Paterson, W.A.R. 114
Pau 80
Perrier Water Assistants Tournament 97, 129, 143-145
Philips, F. 82
Portmarnock 96, 98
Portrush 90
Prestwick 16, 26, 59, 83, 88, 103, 111, 116
prices *see* costs; balls
prize money 7, 94, 96, 98-99, 103, 107, 108, 110, 129, 136-137, 143, 144-145, 149, 151, 153, 154, 166-167
pro-am tournaments
Professional Golfers' Association 26, 33, 39, 40, 93
benevolent fund 40
Employment Agency 40
England v. Scotland matches 83
London Foursomes 146, 147
Open Championship 114-115, 117, 120-121, 124-128
Perrier Water Assistants' Tournament 143
Tooting Bec Cup 140
professional status 31, 36-38
professional teams 54-55, 89
professionals employed by gentlemen 35
Pulford, George 107, 115

Purley Downs 142, 143

railways 11-12
Rainford, Peter 71, 83, 84, 137
Ray, Ted 9, 43, 70, 72, 95, 100, 102, 123
earnings 166
England v. Scotland matches 83, 84, 86, 87, 88, 90
in America 78-80
in Europe 81, 149, 150, 152, 153, 154
London Foursomes 147
News of the World Tournament 130, 131, 132, 134, 135, 136
Open Championships 110, 116, 120, 121, 122, 124
point averages 159-164
Sphere and *Tatler* Cups 138, 139
Tooting Bec Cup 143
Reid, A.E. 97
Reid, Wilfrid 90, 95, 97, 137, 141, 142, 146, 147, 149, 153
Renouf, Tom G. 83, 84, 86, 89, 90, 128
Riddell, George 57, 64
Ritchie, W.L. 143
Roberts, C.T. 137
Robson, Fred 87, 89, 102, 116, 132, 136, 137, 147-148, 159-160
Rolland, Douglas 9, 57, 58, 104, 158
Rome 81, 82
Romford 140
Rosedale, Toronto 75
Rowe, Jack 83, 84, 126, 133, 135
Royal and Ancient 16, 103
Rules of Golf Committee 8, 27
see also St Andrews
Royal Golf Club de Belgique 151-152
Royal Liverpool 16, 103
Spring Medal (1902) 21
see also Hoylake
Royal Montreal 75
Royal North Devon 116
Royal St George's 103, 113
see also Sandwich
rules of the game 8
(1909) 28
about balls 26-27
about clubs 28, 30
Ryder Cup 132
Ryle, Arthur 38

St Andrews 25, 47, 58, 59, 60, 61, 64, 65, 88, 104, 110, 113, 118, 119
St Anne's 15, 16, 66
St Augustine, Florida 74
St Jean de Luz 82
St Lawrence Harbour, New Jersey 74
Sandwich 9, 16, 58, 61, 62, 70, 84, 89, 103, 104, 108, 112, 119, 158
Sandy Lodge 27
San Pedro de los Pinos 77
Sayers, Ben 9, 34, 36, 43, 58, 59, 60, 61, 71, 72, 91
in Europe 81, 82, 149
London Foursomes 147

175

News of the World Tournament 130
Open Championships 106, 116
point average 159
Scotland v. England matches 83, 84, 85, 86, 88, 89, 90
Scotland v. Ireland matches 90
Sphere and *Tatler* Cups 137
Sayers, Ben, Jnr 88, 147
Schenectady putters 28
Scotland v. England matches 83-90
Scotland v. Ireland matches 90
Scott, A.H. 59, 112
Scottish Golf Union 97
Sherlock, James 71, 102
England v. Scotland matches 83, 84, 85, 86, 87
in Europe 82, 151, 152
News of the World Tournament 134, 135
Open Championships 113, 115, 126
Sphere and *Tatler* Cups 137
Tooting Bec Cup 142
Simpson, Archie 58, 60, 90, 144
in Europe 80
Smith, Alex 87, 92
Smith, George 139
Smith, Ralph 83, 84, 85, 88, 90, 112, 115, 126, 140, 147
Smith, Tom 75
Smith, Willie 74, 77, 118
Spalding golf balls 73
spectators 47-48, 59, 66, 68
Sphere Cup 93, 94, 97, 98, 99, 129, 136-139, 170
number of players 148
sports associations 12
Stoke Poges 71, 142, 147
Stuart, Alexander 36
subscriptions 16
Sudbrook Park, Richmond 59
suffragettes 156
Sunningdale 62, 71, 72, 129, 130, 132, 134, 135, 139, 146
Sussex Golfing Union 98
Sykes, Sir Charles 51

Tait, Freddie 35, 36, 91, 106
Tatler Cup 93, 94, 97, 98, 99, 129, 136-139, 170
number of players 148
Taylor, J.H. 7, 9, 22, 30, 33, 34, 35-36, 43, 48, 55, 56, 58, 59, 60, 61, 62, 69, 70, 92, 95, 99, 100, 101, 126, 158
and Golf Professionals' War Fund 155
and Professional Golfers' Association 39, 40
background 31
course design 81
earnings 44, 94, 166
England v. Scotland matches 83, 84, 85, 86, 87, 88, 89, 90
in America 75-77
in Europe 80-82, 149, 150, 152, 154
London Foursomes 146, 147
News of the World Tournament 130, 131, 132, 134, 136
on club-making by professionals 38
on sales of balls by professionals 41
Open Championships 104, 105-106, 107, 108, 109, 110, 112, 113, 114, 115, 116, 117, 120, 122, 124, 126, 128
point averages 159-165
Sphere and *Tatler* Cups 137
Tooting Bec Cup 140, 141, 142
training 51
see also Four Greens Foursome Match (1905)
Taylor, Joshua 138, 139, 147
Taylor, P.E. 138
Taylor, Percy 75, 76
team matches 54-55
England v. Scotland 83-90
Tellier, Louis 81, 92, 150
Thomson, Robert 83, 84, 85, 86, 88, 113
Thorpe Hall 143
Tillinghast, A.W. 79
Timperley 31-32, 68
Tingey, Albert 80-81, 83, 84, 85, 86, 147
Toogood, Alfred H. 58, 86, 90, 104, 131, 141, 146
Toogood, Walter 83, 84, 113, 116
Tooting Bec 15, 16
Tooting Bec Cup 97, 139, 140-143
Totteridge 141, 144
tournaments 93-102
training 51
Tranmore 90
transport 11-12
Travis, Walter 18, 28, 77, 141
Troon 59, 60, 65, 126-127
Turnberry 92
Turner, J. 147

U.S.A. tours 73-79
US v. France match (1913) 92
US Open Championship 74, 75, 76, 78, 95

Vardon, Harry 9, 22, 23, 27, 33, 34, 35-36, 43, 45, 48, 49, 50, 54, 56, 58, 59, 60, 61, 62, 68, 70, 91, 92, 95, 99, 100, 101, 102
and Northern Counties Professional Golfers' Association 39
background 31
clothing 52, 53
earnings 41, 44, 94, 166
England v. Scotland matches 83, 84, 85, 86, 87, 89, 90
in America 73, 75, 78-80
in Europe 80, 81, 83, 149, 150, 151, 152, 153, 154
London Foursomes 147
News of the World Tournament 130, 131, 132, 133, 134, 135, 136
on club-making by professionals 38
Open Championships 104, 106, 107, 108, 109, 110, 111, 112, 113, 114, 115, 116, 120, 121, 122, 128
point averages 159-165

Sphere and *Tatler* Cups 137, 139
Tooting Bec Cup 142, 143
training 51
see also Four Greens Foursome Match (1905)
Vardon, Tom 27, 31, 62, 70
England v. Scotland matches 83, 84, 86, 87, 88
in Europe 80-81, 83, 149, 151, 152
London Foursomes 147
News of the World Tournament 131, 132
Open Championships 113
Tooting Bec Cup 142
"Vardon Flyer" golf balls 73
Varenna 80
Veness, E. 102

Walton Heath 31, 68, 70, 71, 72, 131, 133, 134, 136, 137, 146
Walton Heath Tournament 99
Watt, Tom 90, 115
Watt, Willie 136, 143
Welsh Championship 97
Welsh Golf Union 97
West Herts 142, 143
West Middlesex 140
Westward Ho! 116
Wheaton, Illinois 75
Whitcombe, Ernest 136
White, Jack 9, 26, 27, 34, 40, 43, 59, 62, 63, 71, 77
earnings 166
England v. Scotland matches 83, 84, 85, 86, 88, 89
in Europe 81
London Foursomes 147
News of the World Tournament 130, 131
on club-making by professionals 38
Open Championships 109, 112, 113, 115
point averages 159, 162-165
Sphere and *Tatler* Cups 137
Tooting Bec Cup 140, 141
Whiting, J.W. 138
Whiting, S. 97, 138
Williamson, Tom 85, 86, 87, 90, 109, 115, 130, 134, 138, 139, 151, 152
Wilson, R.G. 135, 136, 137, 139
Wingate, Charlie 102
Witley Court 34
Woking 146
Work, Bertram 18
wry-necked clubs 30
Wynne, 147

Yeoman, T. 86
Yorkshire Professional Foursomes 99
Yorkshire Union of Golf Clubs 98